The
Russian
Americans

Consulting Editors

THE IMMIGRANT EXPERIENCE

The
Russian
Americans

Paul R. Magosci

Sandra Stotsky, General Editor
Harvard University Graduate School of Education

CHELSEA HOUSE PUBLISHERS

New York • Philadelphia

CHELSEA HOUSE PUBLISHERS

Editorial Director: Richard Rennert
Executive Managing Editor: Karyn Gullen Browne
Copy Chief: Robin James
Picture Editor: Adrian G. Allen
Creative Director: Robert Mitchell
Art Director: Joan Ferrigno
Production Manager: Sallye Scott

THE IMMIGRANT EXPERIENCE

Editors: Rebecca Stefoff and Reed Ueda

Staff for THE RUSSIAN AMERICANS

Assistant Editor: Annie McDonnell
Copy Editor: Apple Kover
Assistant Designer: Stephen Schildbach
Cover Illustrator: Jane Sterrett

First Printing

1 3 5 7 9 8 6 4 2

Library of Congress Cataloging-in-Publication Data

Magocsi, Paul R.
    The Russian Americans / Paul R. Magocsi : Sandra Stotsky, general editor.
    p. cm.—(The immigrant experience)
    Includes bibliographical references (p.) and index.
    ISBN 0-7910-3367-8.
        0-7910-3389-9 (pbk.)
    1. Russian Americans—Juvenile literature. I. Stotsky, Sandra. II. Title. III. Series.
E184.R9M36   1995   95-12599
973′.049171—dc20   CIP

CONTENTS

THE IMMIGRANT EXPERIENCE

CHELSEA HOUSE PUBLISHERS

A
NATION OF
NATIONS

Daniel Patrick Moynihan

The Constitution of the United States begins: "We the People of the United States. . ." Yet, as we know, the United States was not then and is not now made up of a single group of people. It is made up of many peoples. Immigrants and bondsmen from Europe, Asia, Africa, and Central and South America came here or were brought here, and still they come. They forged one nation and made it their own. More than 100 years ago, Walt Whitman expressed this great central fact of America: "Here is not merely a nation, but a teeming Nation of nations."

Although the ingenuity and acts of courage of these immigrants, our ancestors, shaped the North American way of life, we sometimes take their contributions for granted. This fine series, *The Peoples of North America*, examines the experiences and contributions of different immigrant groups and how these contributions determined the future of the United States and Canada.

Immigrants did not abandon their ethnic traditions when they reached the shores of North America. Each ethnic group had its own customs and traditions, and each brought different experiences, accomplishments, skills, values, styles of dress, and tastes in food that lingered long after its arrival. Yet this profusion of differences created a singularity, or bond, among the immigrants.

The United States and Canada are unusual in this respect. Whereas religious and ethnic differences have sparked intolerance throughout the rest of the world—from the 17th-century religious wars to the 19th-century nationalist movements in Europe to the near extermination of the Jewish people under Nazi Germany—North Americans have struggled to learn how to respect each other's differences and live in harmony.

Our two countries are hardly the only two in which different groups must learn to live together. There is no nation of significant size anywhere in the world which would not be classified as multi-ethnic. But only in North America are there so *many* different groups, most of them living cheek by jowl with one another.

This is not easy. Look around the world. And it has not always been easy for us. Witness the exclusion of Chinese immigrants, and for practical purposes Japanese also, in the late 19th century. But by the late 20th century, Chinese and Japanese Americans were the most successful of all the groups recorded by the census. We have had prejudice aplenty, but it has been resisted and recurrently overcome.

The remarkable ability of Americans to live together as one people was seriously threatened by the issue of slavery. Thousands of settlers from the British Isles had arrived in the colonies as indentured servants, agreeing to work for a specified number of years on farms or as apprentices in return for passage to America and room and board. When the first Africans arrived in the then-British colonies during the 17th century, some colonists thought that they too should be treated as indentured servants. Eventually, the question of whether the Africans should be treated as inden-tured, like the English, or as slaves who could be owned for life was considered in a Maryland court. The court's calamitous decree held that blacks were slaves bound to a lifelong servitude, and so also were their children. America went through a time of moral ex-amination and civil war before it finally freed African slaves and their descendants. The principle that all people are created equal had faced its greatest challenge and survived.

Yet the court ruling that set blacks apart from other races fanned flames of discrimination that burned long after slavery was abolished—and that still flicker today. Indeed, it was about the time of the American Civil War that European theories of evolution were turned to the service of ranking different peoples by their presumed distance from our apelike ancestors.

When the Irish flooded American cities to escape the famine in Ireland, the cartoonists caricatured the typical "Paddy" (a common term for Irish immigrants) as an apelike creature with jutting jaw and sloping forehead.

By the 20th century, racism and ethnic prejudice had given rise to virulent theories of a Northern European master race. When Adolf Hitler came to power in Germany in 1933, he popularized the notion of an Aryan race. Only a man of the deepest ignorance and evil could have done this. *Aryan* is a Sanskrit word, which is to say the ancient script of what we now think of as India. It means "noble" and was adopted by linguists—notably by a fine German scholar, Max Müller—to denote the Indo-European family of languages. Müller was horrified that anyone could think of it in terms of race, especially a race of blond-haired, blue-eyed Teutons. But the Nazis embraced the notion of a master race. Anyone with darker and heavier features was considered inferior. Buttressed by these theories, the German Nazi state from 1933 to 1945 set out to destroy European Jews, along with Poles, Gypsies, Russians, and other groups considered inferior. It nearly succeeded. Millions of these people were murdered.

The tragedies brought on by ethnic and racial intolerance throughout the world demonstrate the importance of North America's efforts to create a society free of prejudice and inequality.

A relatively recent example of the New World's desire to resolve ethnic friction nonviolently is the solution that the Canadians found to a conflict between two ethnic groups. A long-standing dispute as to whether Canadian culture was properly English or French resurfaced in the mid-1960s, dividing the peoples of the French-speaking Province of Quebec from those of the English-speaking provinces. Relations grew tense, then bitter, then violent. The Royal Commission on Bilingualism and Biculturalism was established to study the growing crisis and to propose measures to ease the tensions. As a result of the commission's recommendations, all official documents and statements from the national government's capital at Ottawa are now issued in both French and English, and bilingual education is encouraged.

The year 1980 marked a coming of age for the United States's ethnic heritage. For the first time, the U.S. Bureau of the Census asked people about their ethnic background. Americans chose from more than 100 groups, including French Basque, Spanish Basque, French Canadian, African-American, Peruvian, Armenian, Chinese, and Japanese. The ethnic group with the largest response was English (49.6 million). More than 100 million Americans claimed ancestors from the British Isles, which includes England, Ireland, Wales, and Scotland. There were almost as many Germans (49.2 million) as English. The Irish-American population (40.2 million) was third, but the next-largest ethnic group, the African-Americans, was a distant fourth (21 million). There was a sizable group of French ancestry (13 million) as well as of Italian (12 million). Poles, Dutch, Swedes, Norwegians, and Russians followed. These groups, and other smaller ones, represent the wondrous profusion of ethnic influences in North America.

Canada too has learned more about the diversity of its population. Studies conducted during the French/English conflict showed that Canadians were descended from Ukrainians, Germans, Italians, Chinese, Japanese, native Indians, and Inuit, among others. Canada found it had no ethnic majority, although nearly half of its immigrant population had come from the British Isles. Canada, like the United States, is a land of immigrants for whom mutual tolerance is a matter of reason as well as principle. But note how difficult this can be in practice, even for persons of manifest goodwill.

The people of North America are the descendants of one of the greatest migrations in history. And that migration is not over.

Koreans, Vietnamese, Nicaraguans, Cubans, and many others are heading for the shores of North America in large numbers. This mix of cultures shapes every aspect of our lives. To understand ourselves, we must know something about our diverse ethnic ancestry. Nothing so defines the North American nations as the motto on the Great Seal of the United States: *E Pluribus Unum*—Out of Many, One.

Since coming to North America in the 1740s, Russians have left the imprint of their language, religion, and culture on the New World. This orchestra—made up of Russians and Eskimos— played in Alaska in the late 19th century.

A MEETING OF TWO CULTURES

The Russians seem to fascinate Americans. Perhaps the source of the fascination is the rivalry that long existed between the two world powers; perhaps it is the great contrast between the two cultures; or perhaps it is Russia's sheer size. For most of the 20th century, Russia was the center of the Soviet Union, an empire larger in size and population than the United States and Canada combined. It may surprise most Americans to learn how many Russian immigrants and their descendants live in North America; estimates place about 750,000 people of Russian descent in the United States and about 50,000 in Canada.

Russians began to arrive on the western coast of North America in the late 18th century. Then, at the end of the 19th and the beginning of the 20th century, the Russians' numbers and impact increased significantly. Thereafter, Russian immigration occurred es-

13

sentially in waves. Each wave was prompted by events that were sweeping across the Russian homeland—economic hardship, religious persecution, civil war, the establishment of the Soviet government, and foreign invasion and displacement by war. (Some participants and historians count the Russian immigration as three waves, some count four; in this book we will observe the majority view that there have been three waves of immigration by persons now called Russian Americans.)

Cross-cultural Dilemmas

Those who came from Russia to the United States between 1917 and 1991 faced a special dilemma. They were proud of their heritage, but because their homeland was ruled by a communist regime unfriendly to the United States, they often faced suspicion and accusations that they were sympathetic to communism, although most had no affection for the communist rulers of the Soviet Union. Some Russian Americans responded to this dilemma by fully adapting to American society. Others strove to maintain their loyalty as American citizens while still holding on to their distinctive cultural heritage. The many Russian Orthodox churches and Russian-language newspapers in North America are two obvious signs of this attempt at cultural preservation.

The efforts of the Russian Americans have had another interesting effect: a cultural exchange. Many Russian immigrants have enriched the American way of life through their artistic, humanistic, and scientific achievements. Among the more well known are ballet master George Balanchine and dancers Mikhail Baryshnikov and Natalia Makarova; Igor Sikorsky, inventor of the helicopter; and writers Vladimir Nabokov and Joseph Brodsky. There are dozens more, many of whom, like Brodsky and Baryshnikov, arrived on these shores as recently as the 1970s, amid a renewed wave of emigration that has enriched both America and the

world. Among this group especially, culture shock manifests itself in their social and creative lives.

What makes the Russian Americans yet more intriguing, aside from their ongoing achievements, is the complexity of the group itself. Because each wave came from differing circumstances, their adjustment to the New World is as much the story of their adjustment to one another as it is of that to their new surroundings.

On the whole, Russian Americans have succeeded so well in adjusting that many of them have assimilated

The Vais family were Soviet citizens who chose to seek asylum in the United States in 1985 for political and religious reasons. Since 1970 a new wave of emigration from the Soviet Union has revitalized Russian-American life.

The political boundaries of Eastern Europe during the cold war.
Russian immigrants have come mainly from the European part of
the former Soviet Union (west of the Ural Mountains), which
represented only about one-quarter of that nation's landmass.

thoroughly the Western styles of work, dress, and ambition. What they have retained of their Russianness is still highly visible in a few of their new neighborhoods, and the difficulties they encounter should teach everyone—American, Canadian, and Russian—something about our contrasting ways of life. ✎

From Medieval Duchy to Superpower

The story of how ethnic Russians, beginning in a small area of eastern Europe, conquered many of the peoples of Europe and Asia and built an empire is a remarkable national history. Russian history figures significantly in almost every Russian immigrant's identity and is a factor in whether the immigrant adapts or feels out of place in his or her new land.

"Russian immigrants" refers to everyone who arrived in America from the Russian Empire (before 1917), the Soviet Union (1917 through 1991), or Russia (since 1991). Roughly half are members of the Russian ethnic group. The others belong to scores of other national and ethnic groups that were part of the Russian Empire or the Soviet Union. These include Slavs (Byelorussians, Ukrainians), Baltic peoples (Estonians, Latvians, Lithuanians), Russian Jews, Caucasians (Armenians, Georgians), and Turkic peoples (Uzbeks, Kazakhs). Other books in this series discuss these ethnic groups. Jews who came from areas under Russian con-

Muscovy and the Russian empire have historically contained scores of different ethnic and national groups, including Ukrainians, Turks, Germans, and Jews.

trol in the 19th and early 20th centuries are covered in the volume on Jewish Americans.

Although atheism was the official policy of the Soviet Union, religion played a part in the life of virtually every national group in Russia—Christianity in the form of Russian Orthodoxy (the historic and dominant faith of Russia), Catholicism, and Protestantism; Judaism, a small and beleaguered faith that has helped shape Russia's culture in the face of periodic outbreaks of anti-Semitism; Buddhism in easternmost Russia; animism or spirit worship in Siberia; and the Muslim faith of Soviet central Asia. More than 100 languages were spoken across the Soviet Union, although the Russian language and culture were foremost in official circles.

Although many people equate Russia with communism, this ideology ruled for only 74 of the nation's 1,000 years. And communism was an import from western Europe. Communism's founders, Karl Marx and Friedrich Engels, were Germans. But Russia was the first state in which an avowedly communist government took power, and its example was followed by many nations.

Kievan Rus' and the Duchy of Muscovy

European Russia (the part of the country west of the Ural Mountains) was occupied by various peoples from about the 2nd millennium B.C., but the main body of Russian history begins in the 9th century A.D. At that time, the rulers of the city of Novgorod began to unite the East Slavic and Finnic tribes in northern Russia with the help of Scandinavian merchants and warriors who came to be known as the *Rus'*. (The name *Rus'* is thought by some to derive from *ruotsi*, the Finnic word for Scandinavian Swedes.)

For decades the Rus' had been trading along the east coast of the Baltic Sea, and in the 860s the local Slavic and Finnic tribes sent an invitation to the Scandinavian leader Rurik:

> Our land is great and rich
> but there is no order in it.
> Come to rule and reign over us.

Rurik accepted the invitation, ruled Novgorod and other nearby trading outposts, and continued to ply the trade routes that connected the Baltic Sea with areas farther south, especially the Black Sea and beyond it the Eastern Roman, or Byzantine, Empire.

The desire for trade with Byzantium brought Rurik's successors southward to Kiev, which by the end of the 9th century was the center of a new state known as *Kievan Rus'*. This medieval state was to last until the

13th century, at its greatest extent covering large parts of what are today the Ukraine, Byelorussia, and European Russia. The city of Kiev ranked among the largest in Europe during the Middle Ages, with perhaps 400 churches adorning its reach.

In fact, it was during the Kievan period that all of the East Slavs (Russians, Byelorussians, Ukrainians) were brought into the fold of Christianity. Linked by trade from its earliest days to the Byzantine Empire, Kievan Rus' received Christianity from that source in the eastern or Byzantine Greek form.

Christianity had acquired some converts among the Rus' already in the 9th century, but it was not until 988 that the ruler of Kiev, Vladimir the Great (ruled, 978–1015), adopted it as the official religion of his domain. After 1054, when the Christian churches split permanently into the western (Roman) and eastern (Orthodox) branches, Kievan Rus' would remain Orthodox.

St. Basil's Cathedral in Moscow, built in the Russo-Byzantine style between 1554 and 1679, symbolizes the lasting power and influence of the Russian Orthodox church, despite the current restrictions on religion in the motherland.

The conversion also brought culture in the form of Byzantine church books translated into the Old Slavonic language via an alphabet invented earlier by the Byzantine missionary St. Cyril. Based on a modified form of Greek letters later known as Cyrillic, this alphabet is still used today by Russians and other East and South Slavs. In recognition of the cultural and spiritual importance of the 988 conversion, in 1988 Russian Orthodox churches in the United States and elsewhere celebrated with great pomp and solemnity the 1,000-year anniversary, or millennium, of what is called the baptism of Rus'.

Like many other medieval states, Kievan Rus' suffered from internal weakness caused by political rivalries and conflicts among its many ruling princes, all of whom claimed descent from Rurik. There was also the constant threat of attack by fierce nomadic tribes, who between the 10th and 13th centuries periodically swept out of central Asia, destroyed much along their path, and then settled in the steppe region north of the Black Sea. From there they would carry on raids against the southern borderlands of Kievan Rus'. The last and most devastating of these central Asian warriors were the Mongols, whose huge armies, composed primarily of Tatar soldiers, attacked and destroyed many cities throughout Kievan Rus' between 1237 and 1241. As Kievan Rus' declined, several Rus' principalities became independent states. Among these was the duchy of Muscovy in the north.

Centered around the city of Moscow, the duchy of Muscovy began its rise to power in the 1300s, and by the end of the century it had become one of the leading principalities in the old Kievan Rus' federation as well as the seat of the Orthodox church. Moscow owed its strength to its strategic location in the heart of northern Russia's river routes (its *kremlin*, or fort, overlooked the Moscow River) and to a series of shrewd and talented leaders. By the end of the 15th century, their goal was to reunite all the lands that had once belonged to Kievan Rus'.

Mongol tribesmen (right) swept into Europe and sacked many of the cities in the Kievan Rus' federation. They also attacked the duchy of Muscovy in the 13th and 14th centuries, but were eventually repulsed by Russians under Ivan III in 1480.

The first challenge to those ambitions came from the Mongols and their Tatar successors, who through a vast empire stretching across central Asia and the southern steppelands continued to exact payment from Muscovy and other Rus' principalities. This period, from about the 1250s to 1480, is still remembered in Russian history as that of the "Tatar yoke."

The second challenge came from the west, where the powerful Grand Duchy of Lithuania and its later ally Poland conquered most of the western and southern lands that had belonged to Kievan Rus'—today's Byelorussia and Ukraine. And the third came from Sweden, which ruled the Baltic Sea and much of what is today Estonia, Latvia, and what would become the region of Leningrad.

The Rise of the Czars

Among the most successful of the Muscovite state builders was Grand Prince Ivan III (ruled, 1462–1505), who succeeded in uniting most of the principalities of northern Rus' and refused to pay tribute to the Tatars. He was the first ruler to claim a unique historic destiny for Muscovy, asserting that Moscow should take the lead in gathering together all the "Russian" lands that had once been part of Kievan Rus'. He also proclaimed himself inheritor of the imperial tradition of Rome and assumed the title *czar* (from the Latin *caesar*).

In 1453 the once-mighty Byzantine Empire and its capital Constantinople (the "Second Rome") fell to the Ottoman Turks. Ivan III, who married the niece of the last Byzantine emperor, now considered himself heir to the imperial Byzantine tradition. His successor, Vasily III (ruled, 1505–33) went one step further, asserting that Muscovy was the "Third Rome." It was also at this time that Muscovy's church became independent. Muscovite churchmen professed that because the mother church in Constantinople was under Islamic Ottoman sway, only their Orthodox church could preserve the "true faith."

Armed with a clear political and religious ideology, Muscovy's rulers set out to "reunite" all those lands once part of Kievan Rus'. The most aggressive and ultimately brutal in this regard was Ivan IV (ruled, 1533–84), also known as the "Dread" or "Terrible." He was the first of Muscovy's rulers to be crowned czar, and he succeeded in destroying the Tatar states in the south. But he also weakened the realm through a costly and unsuccessful attempt to win back the Baltic region and by the suppression of his opponents among the *boyars*, or landed aristocrats.

Ivan IV's reign was followed by a 30-year period of internal anarchy and foreign invasion known as the Time of Troubles. This critical period was immortalized in the 19th century by Modest Mussorgsky's opera *Boris Godunov* (based on the play by Alexander Pushkin), named for the hapless czar who ruled for part of this time.

Peace and stability began to be restored in 1613 when Michael Romanov (ruled, 1613–45) was elected czar by a boyar council. The Romanov family would rule Muscovy and later the Russian empire until the fall of the last czar in 1917. It was during the reign of Michael and his son Alexis (ruled, 1645–76) that peasant laborers were forbidden, after 1649, to leave the estates to which they were bound. So was born *serfdom*, a system of modified slavery that locked millions of peasant serfs into impoverished servitude. The rigid class system in Muscovy and the Russian empire, based on control of serfs by a small group of aristocratic landowners, would not change appreciably until 1861, when the serfs were freed.

In the 17th century came another important turning point. Muscovy's foremost enemies to the west — Poland-Lithuania and Sweden — began to decline, and in 1654 Muscovy was able to gain from Poland the eastern Ukraine and the historically symbolic city of Kiev. The same era also witnessed Muscovy's rapid advance across Siberia. That push, begun in 1581, took the Muscovites to the Pacific Ocean in less than a century.

With Michael Romanov's ascension to czar in 1613, Muscovy began 300 years of autocracy under one family. The primacy of the monarchy — and the reach of the Russian empire — expanded but finally gave way because of Romanov misrule.

The biggest changes, however, came during the reign of Peter I (the Great, ruled, 1682–1725), who was determined to modernize Muscovy and bring it up to the standards of contemporary western Europe. He completely reorganized the country's governmental structure and in 1721 was proclaimed emperor, at which time Muscovy was renamed Russia.

Peter was enamored with the sea (he had worked a year incognito in a shipyard in Holland), and he was determined to gain permanent seaports for Russia. In the south, he carried on costly wars with the Turks for access to the Black Sea, but was ultimately unsuccessful. His luck was better along the Baltic Sea, where after winning the Great Northern War (1700–21) against Sweden he was able to acquire most of what is today Estonia and Latvia.

Symbolic of Peter's thrust to the sea and Westernization of the country was his decision in 1703 to build a new capital—a "window to the West"—where the Neva River flows into the Gulf of Finland. He built the new city, called St. Petersburg, entirely in the architectural styles of western Europe, rejecting the old Muscovite ways. St. Petersburg (today called Leningrad)

Peter the Great (reigned 1682–1725), one of the most dynamic czars, sought greater contact with western Europe. He ordered the building of a new imperial capital, St. Petersburg, where the Neva River reaches the Gulf of Finland.

Catherine II (the Great) completed the quest for European territory that Czar Peter was unable to achieve. Part of her legacy was the interest she took in Russian exploration of North America.

remains an island of western European cultural influence in Russia and a prime tourist attraction in the Soviet Union. Peter not only transformed medieval Muscovy into the Russian empire; his actions also set the stage for a later controversy in Russian thought: On one side were those who favored turning toward the West for inspiration and models of social change; on the other were those who favored more traditional, native "Russian" ways.

Much of what Peter hoped to achieve in foreign affairs was completed some decades later by Empress Catherine II (the Great, ruled, 1762–96). It was during Catherine's reign that the Russian empire finally gained the warm-water ports it had long coveted from the Ot-

Under Napoleon (front, in white breeches), the French Grand Army advanced to the gates of Moscow in 1812. The czarist army and a cruel Russian winter proved an unbeatable combination that spelled the eventual ruin of the "Little Corporal's" empire.

toman Empire—the Crimean peninsula and the shore of the Black Sea. The most important addition was the new city of Odessa, founded in the 1790s. Catherine also oversaw the three partitions of Poland, thereby wiping that country entirely off the map in 1795 and making Russia the largest European land power. And she supported the first attempts—by hunters and missionaries—to stake out the part of Alaska and Canada then known as Russian America.

Territorial Growth and Economic Backwardness

The Russian empire's stance as a major European power posed a challenge to the French emperor Napoleon, who had already subjugated most of the Continent. In 1812 he decided to conquer Russia, but a severe winter and a hostile response by the Russian military and populace caused France's "grand campaign" to end in complete failure. The brief but eventful Napoleonic era in Russian history was immortalized in Leo Tolstoy's novel *War and Peace* and through Peter Tchaikovsky's stirring musical work, the *1812 Overture* (still often played in America at Fourth of July festivities).

With Napoleon's demise in 1815, the Russian empire was in an even stronger position than before. It had annexed Finland in 1809, and then, by treaty, gained the rest of Poland in 1815. The country was now able to turn its attention eastward: It absorbed Transcaucasia, central Asia, and the Amur and Pacific maritime provinces near China. With these conquests, the Russian empire came to equal one-sixth of the land surface of the globe.

Whether describing aristocratic life, praising the simple strength of the peasantry, or espousing his own religious and moral philosophy, Count Leo Tolstoy (1828–1910) captured the Russian spirit in its essence.

The enormous territorial growth over the centuries brought numerous non-Russian peoples under Russian rule. They were fellow Slavs, Baltic and Finnic peoples, Caucasian peoples, and Siberian and Turkic peoples. Another group was the Jews, most of whom came under Russian rule during the late 18th-century partitions of Poland and who by 1900 numbered about 5 million. In fact, the Russian government passed laws that required Jews to remain within the newly acquired lands, an area that came to be known as the Pale of Settlement, which encompassed most of the area along the empire's western border, what is today much of Poland, Lithuania, Byelorussia, and the Ukraine west of the Dnieper River. In the Pale, the Jews tended to congregate in towns and cities, although many lived in villages where they had their own distinct communities, known in their native tongue, Yiddish, as *shtetls*. Most of the village Jews were poor, as is evident in the humorous stories of Sholem Aleichem, one of which became the basis for the popular Broadway musical *Fiddler on the Roof*.

Although the Russian empire expanded its borders in the 19th century, at the same time it faced widespread poverty and economic backwardness at home. An attempt to remedy the situation came during the reign of Alexander II (ruled, 1855–81), who in the 1860s pushed through a series of social, administrative,

Even at its height as a world power, czarist Russia remained an underdeveloped, backward nation, rife with illiteracy, indigence, and hunger.

educational, and legal reforms, including the liberation of the serfs. However, Alexander's social experiments came to a halt with his assassination in 1881 and the rule of reactionary successors for the rest of the empire's existence.

In essence, the last decades of the 19th century were marked by unresolved social problems, an economy fallen far behind the rest of Europe's, and the rise of revolutionary movements, including the Marxist variety of socialism. The czarist government often responded by arresting suspected political enemies and deporting them to Siberia. There were also rumors spread about enemies still within the country, and these accusations sometimes led to *pogroms*, indiscriminate attacks against Jews, especially in 1881, 1903, 1905, and 1919.

Despite the extreme social inequality and political repression in the latter half of the 19th century, Russian culture experienced a golden age that produced many monumental cultural figures. Though Americans may know little of Russian history, they have quite possibly read a short story by Nikolai Gogol or Ivan Turgenev, a novel by Leo Tolstoy or Fyodor Dostoyevsky, seen a play by Anton Chekhov, or heard the music of Peter Tchaikovsky, Modest Mussorgsky, or Alexander Borodin.

Failed Reform Leads to Revolution

The czarist government of Nicholas II (ruled, 1894–1917) made a concerted effort to industrialize the country and to introduce limited political reform. We will never know whether these efforts would have changed the course of Russian development, however, because in August 1914 Russia entered World War I. She joined her allies France, Great Britain, and later the United States, who were pitted against the Central Powers—Germany, Austria-Hungary, and Ottoman Turkey. But the Russian empire was ill prepared for war and suffered 5.5 million dead or wounded.

Dramatist Anton Chekhov (1860–1904), whose finest works include The Cherry Orchard *and* The Three Sisters, *lived during Russia's greatest cultural epoch—the late 19th century. He accurately perceived that the nobility was doomed by its own stagnation.*

The end of an era: Czar Nicholas II and his five children fled their palace but were seized and sent into exile. Later the czar's family and hundreds of other nobles were executed by Bolsheviks.

The strain of the war on an already weak economy proved to be too much, and in early 1917 protests against economic hardship and political repression erupted into the Russian Revolution and the overthrow of the czar. In the new political environment, many long-suppressed, underground revolutionary movements were able to resurface. Among these was the Socialist Revolutionary party, one faction of which was the Bolsheviks. The Provisional Government that had replaced the czar in February was itself overthrown by the Bolsheviks in November, and the Bolsheviks set out to create the world's first *soviet* (workers' council) state.

The New Soviet State

Led by a fervent and talented revolutionary, Vladimir Lenin (1870–1924), the new Soviet state was determined to transform all aspects of Russian society: Communism was to become the social ideal, in which every citizen was ostensibly equal. There was to be no private ownership of land, factories, or shops; instead, they were to be operated by the workers themselves as part of the new workers' state. The Bolsheviks also pulled Russia out of World War I because they considered it to be a conflict between imperialist powers that was being conducted at the expense of Europe's working classes. Thus, the motives behind the Russian Revolution were twofold: to overthrow the corrupt and outmoded autocracy and to end Russia's involvement in the war.

The Bolsheviks' radical approach profoundly disrupted Russian society, leading to a civil war between late 1917 and early 1921. It pitted the Bolshevik "Reds" against the anti-Bolshevik "Whites," those who remained loyal to the old czarist regime or who were simply opposed to Lenin's Bolsheviks. In the end the "Whites" lost, prompting a mass exodus of the rich and those who had served in the czarist administration. Some workers who were unable or unwilling to live in their homeland under its radically changed circumstances also decided to flee. The leading nations of the world granted official recognition to the new state by 1924, after initial doubts about whether the Bolsheviks could maintain a hold on their power. The United States held back recognition until 1933.

The Bolshevik regime survived the civil war (losing some western territories in the process), and in December 1922 the country was renamed the Union of Soviet

One cause of the revolution was the imperial government's inept conduct of World War I, which led to widespread famine as well as military defeat. These children fled to a refugee camp.

Socialist Republics (USSR), or Soviet Union. It comprised not only Soviet Russia but also several other republics, such as the Soviet Ukraine, Soviet Byelorussia, Soviet Armenia, and Soviet Georgia. (Today there are 15 republics in all.) These republics were created in part to fulfill the desires for independence expressed by the old empire's many nationalities during the years of revolution and civil war.

Uniting the country politically and socially was a slow process. After Lenin's death in 1924 and a prolonged struggle for succession, Joseph Stalin (1879–1953) emerged in 1928 as the undisputed Soviet leader. As part of the so-called Stalinist revolution, the country was industrialized under a series of highly ambitious yet unrealistic five-year plans; the agricultural sector was collectivized, meaning that most farms came to be jointly operated under government supervision.

In this process, land was forcibly taken from individual peasant farmers and combined with collective or state farms. Many of the better-off peasants (called *kulaks*) resisted, some by burning their crops and slaughtering their livestock. Stalin launched a drive to "liquidate the kulaks." By the mid-1930s several million people from the rural areas (especially the Ukraine,

A workers' revolt in 1905 tolled the beginning of the revolutionary fervor that culminated in the Russian Revolution of 1917. In that year, the Social Democrat "Reds," whose red flag served as a call to arms, ousted the royalist "Whites."

Vladimir Lenin (left) led the Bolshevik party in its government takeover in November 1917 and its subsequent victory in the civil war. Shortly after Lenin's death in 1924, Joseph Stalin (right) took over and began an aggressive plan to industrialize the nation and collectivize its farms.

the lower Volga valley, and the northern Caucasus region) had been sent to labor camps in Siberia or had died in the deportation or the 1933 famine. The famine victims received little or no help from the government.

War on the Horizon

No sooner had Stalin's government changed the country's economic base than the Soviet Union faced the threat of a new military conflict brewing in Europe. In an effort to stand clear of another European war, the Soviet Union signed a "friendship" treaty in August 1939 with Adolf Hitler's Nazi Germany. The German-Soviet pact also outlined the two countries' respective spheres of influence in eastern Europe, so that when

Hitler's armies invaded Poland from the west on September 1, the Soviet Union was able to expand its own borders into eastern Poland, the Baltic states, and into eastern Romania the following year.

In June 1941, however, Hitler broke his nonaggression pact with Stalin and launched an all-out attack on the Soviet Union. For the next three years large parts of the country's western territories were exposed to the destructive brutality of the war and the German occupation, but Hitler's invasion eventually proved to be one of the greatest strategic blunders in military history. If the Nazis had not been tied up on the eastern front after June 1941, they could have used most of their might on the western front, probably with dire consequences for the Allies.

People in much of the conquered Soviet territory did not resist the Germans' advance at first, seeing in the Nazis their chance for liberation from Soviet rule. But the Nazis quickly proved no more interested in the nationalist sentiments of the Ukrainians or Byelorussians than the Soviets had been.

As in World War I, the Soviet Union was the hardest hit of all the combatants. During the 4 years of conflict from 1941 to 1945 it lost an estimated 11 million soldiers and 7 million civilians. At the costly Battle of Stalingrad (October 1942–February 1943), which proved to be the turning point of the Soviet war effort, one conservative estimate put the Red Army's losses at 500,000 men—more than the United States lost in all battles on all fronts throughout the entire war.

In addition to the enormous military casualties of World War II, hundreds of thousands of Soviet citizens were deported to work in Germany. Thousands more fled westward rather than face the return of Soviet rule. The result was that at the end of the war, Russians and other Soviet nationalities were scattered throughout central and western Europe as well as other parts of the world.

During World War II, the Soviet Union suffered the heaviest losses of any nation, just as it had in World War I. At the Battle of Stalingrad (October 1942–February 1943), the city on the Volga River was destroyed—but the Red Army turned back the Nazis' offensive.

The Making of a Superpower

By mid-1944, the Soviet Union, as one of the five Allies (along with China, France, Great Britain, and the United States), began to drive the armies of Nazi Germany and its allies out of Soviet territory. By the war's end in 1945, the Soviet Union was able to regain all of its former territory, including those lands (eastern Poland, the Baltic states, eastern Romania) acquired at the outset of the war in 1939–40. It also added the small Czechoslovakian province of Subcarpathian Rus' (Transcarpathia). With this last acquisition, the Soviet Union finally fulfilled what had been the centuries-long goal of both Muscovy and the Russian empire: to reunite all the lands once belonging to medieval Kievan Rus'.

This billboard announces a Communist Party Congress in Moscow in 1971. In the Soviet Union the Communist party was the preeminent power; all social, political, and economic matters came under its jurisdiction.

Stalin was hailed as the savior of the Soviet Union during its "great patriotic war," and he presided over its economic recovery. He resumed the policy of centralized planning (with the state in full control of the economy) initiated in 1928. Political repression continued.

The Soviet Union not only expanded its boundaries, it exported its own variety of communism to most countries of central Europe, dominating East Germany, Poland, Czechoslovakia, Hungary, Romania, Bulgaria, and for a while, Yugoslavia, Albania, and, outside of Europe, China. Thus, the Soviet Union, with its expanding sphere of influence, became a world superpower, second only to the United States in military strength.

Soon after the war, the alliance that had been forged with the Americans against Nazi Germany broke down, and since 1945 the Soviet Union's relations with the United States have taken the form of a dangerous superpower rivalry. The hostility is marked alternately by the "cold" war, conducted with spies, diplomats, and propaganda issued from both sides, and by indirect "hot," or shooting, wars, as in Korea, Vietnam, and Afghanistan. Both sides also stockpile military hardware in a maddening arms race and map out hypothetical plans to conquer the world beyond in the exploration of outer space.

The dangerous postwar Soviet-American rivalry eased from time to time in periods of lessened tension called *détente*. One such period occurred during the 1970s, when Russian and American leaders signed arms treaties and initiated cultural exchanges. These same years also witnessed a relaxation in the regulation of people's movements. A new wave of emigrants left the Soviet Union, many of them coming to the United States.

Tension between the two superpowers was further reduced in 1985 with the coming to power of a new Soviet leader, Mikhail Gorbachev. He introduced political and economic reforms so sweeping that they led to the collapse of the Soviet Union in 1991. Various Soviet republics became independent nations, statues of Lenin were toppled from their bases, and Leningrad returned to its precommunist name, St. Petersburg, as did other Russian cities. In the mid-1990s, communism no longer rules Russia. The country is struggling to rebuild its shattered economy with aid from the West and to create a cohesive new social order. Travel into and out of Russia has grown much easier, both for emigrants and for Russians living abroad who wish to visit their homeland. ❧

This family of Old Believers, dissenters from Russian Orthodoxy, now lives in Oregon. There they uphold the traditions of their forebears.

REACHING BEYOND RUSSIA

Russians have maintained a presence on North American soil for longer than most European peoples—more than 240 years. Though their numbers have never been large here, the Russians helped to shape the continent's landscape and development, from Alaska to Florida, in farms and factories, and through public life.

Who exactly are the Russian Americans? Estimating the population of North Americans with Russian roots is problematic because the term *Russian* was originally applied to many immigrants who came from the multinational Russian empire and Soviet Union. These people were in many cases actually Jews, Poles, Byelorussians, Ukrainians, Germans, or others.

According to the 1980 U.S. census, 2,780,000 persons from Russia or the Soviet Union live in the United States, just more than 1 percent of the population. But a more realistic view suggests there are only about 750,000 Americans of *ethnic* Russian descent, meaning they either were born in Russia or have at least one parent or grandparent of ethnic Russian heritage. Much the same difficulty in identifying ethnic Russians applies to Canada, too, though in smaller degree, as fewer immigrants from Russia or the USSR settled in Canada. A 1981 Canadian census showed that about 50,000 Canadians claim Russian ancestry.

From Siberia to Alaska

In 1727 Vitus Bering, a Danish sea captain in the service of the Russian czar, discovered the waters dividing Asia and America that still bear his name—the Bering Sea and Bering Strait. Fourteen years later he landed on the Aleutian Islands, the archipelago that juts southwestward from the Alaskan coast. It was here that the first Russians in the New World settled.

At the time of Bering's discovery, the Russian empire was largely a frontier society, with much of Siberia's enormous expanse still unmapped. Russian traders and adventurers set out over the Siberian wilderness, some pushing as far east as the Pacific Ocean. At first what drew them across the strait to North America were furs and hides—bear, seal, walrus, wolf, beaver, and especially sea otter. Within 20 years of Captain Bering's first landing, Russians were hunting annually on the Aleutians, and by the 1790s they were also plying the waters off the coast of British Columbia. The trading possibilities were tremendous, and the first permanent Russian settlement was founded in 1784 (a year after the American colonies won their revolutionary war) on Kodiak, a large island off the Alaskan mainland. A few years later the village of Yakutat was established on the southeastern coastline.

The fur and hide trade first attracted Russians to North America in the 18th century. Walrus, beaver, and especially sea otter were the basis of the Russian American Company's interests in Alaska and Canada.

By 1800, all settlement and economic activity in the region were directed by the Russian-American Company, whose main interest was the fur trade but whose local power extended into many fields. Their search for the headwaters of the Yukon River took them into Canada, then a British colony, and later in the century the gold rush in the Klondike would also take Russians east from Alaska. In 1812 hunters and settlers pushed south into what is today California and founded Fort Ross, about 100 miles north of San Francisco. Only the Spanish and the British preceded the Russians among European explorers in the California area.

The early Russian presence on the Aleutians and in Alaska and California was temporary and minimal. At its height the Alaskan colony consisted of perhaps 400 Russians, and their numbers dwindled as Americans moved westward. First, Fort Ross was sold in 1841 to Captain John Sutter (on whose land gold was discovered in 1848); then in 1867, the Russian government sold Alaska to the United States for $7.2 million, roughly 2 cents per acre. About half the Russians returned home, and many others set out for the colony in California.

The United States bought Alaska from Czar Alexander II in 1867 for $7.2 million. At the time, many Americans considered the purchase a blunder, but the deal worked out to about two cents per acre.

The longest-lasting influence of the Russians in Alaska and northern Canada was the Orthodox religion. This church in Sitka, Alaska, was the most elaborate built on the frontier.

The sale of all of what had been called Russian America put an end to most of the Russian migration, for the time being.

A more lasting influence than the trading posts was the Russian Orthodox faith, for the fur traders were soon followed into the region by Russian missionaries intent upon baptizing the native Aleuts as Christians. One of them, Father Ioann Veniaminov (1797–1879), invented an alphabet for the Aleut language and published its first dictionary, grammar, Bible, and prayer books. The Orthodox congregation became so large that in 1840 the mother church set up a new diocese for western North America, with Veniaminov as bishop. By the mid-19th century, perhaps 12,000 native Aleutians and Eskimos had been converted to Russian Orthodoxy, sometimes under threat of losing their hunting rights on land newly claimed by the Russians.

Today, the faith is still practiced by Aleuts and many Alaskan Eskimos. The Russian Orthodox church at Sitka, Alaska, is the most elaborate of the edifices left by the missionary era, and smaller churches dot the Alaskan and Yukon terrain as well. Most are the oldest buildings in their town, and a few contain sacred relics (icons and chalices, for instance) brought from prerevolutionary Russia.

Though the Russian presence in North America began in Alaska and the West Coast, it was in the eastern United States that most were to settle. A few individuals had already arrived not long after the colonies became a republic, and their fortunes were as varied as the frontier: Prince Demetrius Gallitzin (1770–1840) landed in Baltimore in 1792, then converted to Catholicism and did missionary work among the Indians of western Pennsylvania; Ivan Turchaninov-Turchin (1822–1901) rose to the rank of brigadier general on the Union side in the American Civil War; Vladimir Stolishnikoff (d. 1907) was a radical political thinker and an architect who helped in the designing of Carnegie Hall; Peter Dementev-Demens (1849–1919) made his way as a railroad builder and cofounded St. Petersburg, Florida, which was named for his birthplace in Russia; and William Frey (born Vladimir K. Gayns, d. 1870), founded utopian communal settlements in Kansas and Oregon that lasted a few years at most. In 1857 a Russian named Alexander Lakier, inspired by Frenchman Alexis de Tocqueville's 1840 account *Democracy in America*, undertook his own examination of the new republic, calling it *A Russian Looks at America*.

The Waves of Immigration

Before the outbreak of World War I in 1914, about 2 million immigrants arrived from the Russian empire. Most of these immigrants belonged to groups that had been persecuted for their religion (Judaism) or nationality (Polish) during the repressive reigns of Alexander III and Nicholas II, even though most had been residing within the empire for generations. In the main, the Jews spoke Yiddish and the Poles spoke Polish. The 1910 U.S. census recorded only 65,000 Russian-speakers from the Russian empire.

By the start of World War I, the number of Russian-speaking persons in the United States had grown to an estimated 100,000. This figure included as many as 50,000 East Slavs from the Austro-Hungarian Empire who converted to Orthodoxy and were consequently identified as Russians. These East Slavs (mostly Ukrainians and Lemkos from Austrian Galicia and Carpatho-Rusyns from Hungary) left to escape the poverty of their homelands, a situation that sent off increasing numbers of them between 1880 and 1910. Like Russians from the Russian empire, the East Slavic "Russians" settled mainly in the industrial areas of New York City, New Jersey, Connecticut, Pennsylvania, and Ohio.

Because of the varied origins of these people, this pre-1914 wave of immigration is largely ignored by Russians who came to the United States in later years. Most historical studies and most Russians themselves enumerate only three waves of Russian immigration to North America: The first wave came during the 1920s and 1930s in the wake of the Russian Revolution; the second wave came in the years immediately following World War II (1945 to the early 1950s); and the immigrants of the third wave have been arriving since the early 1970s.

In the Wake of Civil War

The first wave of immigration surged to the East Coast after the Russian Revolution and civil war of 1917–21.

Violent revolts, property destruction, and political radicalism erupted across the empire, forging the Soviet state and forcing nearly 2 million citizens to flee. Most were former czarist government officials, aristocrats, industrialists, shopkeepers, teachers, lawyers, doctors, military personnel, or churchmen. Although the majority settled in Europe, mainly France and Germany (and especially in Paris, the historic home away from home for Russians), about 30,000 came to the United States under the auspices of the Red Cross, which helped in the major resettlement program.

This number quickly grew. In the 1930s, several thousand Russian refugees fled Europe as Nazism began to engulf the Continent. Because many of these immigrants came from the wealthy ruling class of old czarist Russia, they gravitated toward jobs similar to their former professions, which could be found in the large urban centers, particularly New York City, Philadelphia, Chicago, and San Francisco. In 1930, for example, approximately 1.15 million persons born in the Russian empire lived in the United States, almost half of them in New York City.

The Yearning for Tradition

Though work and comradeship were available in American cities, some immigrants preferred a less congested environment. Before World War II, Russia was largely a rural society, so some newcomers established vibrant rural communities. In New Jersey, for example, one group of pre–World War I Russian immigrants created the 1,400-acre Rova Farm (named for a Russian-American fraternal society), which still flourishes today. During the 1930s, Russians from the Don Cossack region (the lower Don River) established many thriving farm communities in southern New Jersey—at Lakewood, Cassville, and Howell. In all, there were about 30,000 Russian-American farmers in 1925, a number that has slowly declined since.

Other Russians who had suffered religious persecution in their homeland hoped that in the New World they could continue to practice their faith and traditional life-styles. Among these were the Molokans, a non-Orthodox religious sect. The Molokans were given their name (literally, "the milk drinkers") in 1765 for their practice of continuing to drink milk during Lent, when strict Orthodox observance calls for abstinence from all meat, fish, and dairy products. They rejected other beliefs of the Orthodox church, too, emphasizing strict Bible and book study rather than elaborate church ritual. During the 18th century some Molokans fled to neighboring Iran.

Then, in the inhospitable climate of the Russian empire during the first decade of the 20th century, a group of about 5,000 Molokans fled the country. Their pacifist beliefs had put them still further into disfavor with the Russian government, which was enforcing its universal military draft with an eye toward war in Europe. Like others before, they settled first in Iran, but between 1904 and 1912 they left for California—especially San Francisco and Los Angeles. In the 1950s, more Molokans arrived from Iran, and today there are about 20,000 members of the sect living in California and a few thousand in Oregon.

The first wave of Russian immigrants included aristocrats and anti-Bolsheviks fleeing the revolution and civil war. These exiles arrived in San Francisco in 1923.

(continued on page 57)

Eₐₛₜ ₘₑₑₜₛ ₩ₑₛₜ

Overleaf: Two Russian Americans celebrate the Fourth of July outside the Gastronom Moscow, a boardwalk eatery in Brooklyn, New York.

An accordionist performs in a club in Brooklyn. The Brighton Beach section of Brooklyn has become an especially vibrant Russian neighborhood.

A sidewalk sign points the way to an upstairs record store offering music "for any taste." Many Russian Americans have retained their language and traditions while embracing many elements of American culture.

A Russian Orthodox priest presides over an Easter ceremony. Orthodox Easter is the church's most joyous and colorful feast day.

Two Russian American women participate in an Orthodox Easter procession. During the communist rule in Russia, many religiously observant Russians came to America to find religious freedom.

Ethnic Russians in the United States and Canada have been strongly influenced by their religion. At the Russian Orthodox cemetery in Spring Valley, New York, families gather for a post-Easter panikhida *to lay wreaths and flowers and to share a meal in honor of their ancestors.*

At a Russian Orthodox wedding on Long Island, New York, the bride and groom carry candles, while attendants hold crowns just above their head until the priest has sanctified the union.

(continued from page 48)

Even before coming to the United States, the Molokans were divided into two factions. The *Priguny*, or Jumpers, descend from a group founded in the 1840s by a self-proclaimed prophet, Maksim Rudometkin, whose writings are collected in a book called *Dukh i zhizn'* (*Spirit of Life*), which along with the Bible forms the basis of their faith. Many scholars have analyzed the California Molokan Jumpers, who seem strange to outsiders because of the emotional outbursts and physical movements (such as twitching and jumping) that often accompany their religious services. Those Molokans who do not accept Rudometkin's teachings (and who do not jump during services) are known as the *Postoiannye*, or the Steadfast Ones. Both groups still practice their faith, with about 17,000 Priguny found mainly in and around Los Angeles and nearly 3,000 Postoiannye in San Francisco.

Other religious groups also sought a safe environment in which to observe their faith. One such group was the Old Believers, who descend from Orthodox Russians who refused to accept the liturgical reforms introduced in the mid-17th century: The Old Believers continued to use the prereform liturgical books, to cross themselves with two instead of three fingers, and to keep their long beards; some groups even rejected the priesthood. Because of these divergences from the official church, the Old Believers were often brutally persecuted and forced to live in remote areas of the Russian empire or to emigrate. There are about 8,000 Old Believers living in the United States today.

About 3,000 Old Believers (mostly from priestless groups) arrived in the United States before World War I from the western regions of the Russian empire (Poland and the Baltic region), where they had previously sought refuge. They settled in the industrial regions around Pittsburgh and especially Erie, Pennsylvania, where they formed extremely tight-knit communities.

A few more Old Believers immigrated after each of the world wars, but the next significantly large group did not arrive until the 1960s, settling in southern New

Countess Eugenia Musin-Pushkin sits at a small table in her home in New Jersey in 1973. An unwilling immigrant in the 1920s, she continued to believe that "the Czar was a good man."

Several thousand Molokans, a religious group persecuted in Russia, came to California between 1904 and 1912. Others arrived in the 1950s, and today more than 20,000 Molokans live in the United States. These people gathered in San Francisco in 1970.

Jersey. Some came from Turkey, where their ancestors had fled from Russia as early as the 1730s. In New Jersey, however, their traditional way of life was quickly undermined by modern influences, more than it had been during generations spent in Turkey. The more devout among them reacted by seeking an isolated, rural existence in the Willamette River valley of Oregon.

Another group of Old Believers has had an even more storm-tossed history. They first left Soviet Russia in the 1920s and 1930s, settling in China and Japan. Then, in the 1950s and 1960s, they moved to Brazil. Shortly thereafter, they joined their brethren in Oregon. Finally, they founded a new settlement in Nikolaevsk, Alaska, where they seem to have found the quietude required for their religion and customs. The comparative isolation there has enabled them to preserve their Russian ethnicity.

The Orthodox Church: Preserving the Old World in the New

As was the case with many other immigrant groups, the Russians' religion served as an anchor in their years of movement. In fact, the Russian Orthodox faith has proved to have a significant influence on their lives in America. Even though Orthodoxy is not the only faith practiced by Russian Americans, it is the one most often associated with the group.

Orthodoxy is one of the three main branches of Christianity, along with Catholicism and Protestantism. The Russian Orthodox religion differs from other Christian faiths, for example, in following the oldest traditions and marking church holidays by the Julian calendar. So feasts such as Christmas fall two weeks later for the Russian Orthodox than for Catholics and Protestants, who follow the Gregorian calendar first adopted in the 16th century. Russian Orthodox Easter

The Stephen Peganoff family, pictured here in 1912, settled in Erie, Pennsylvania, along with many other Old Believers.

is the church's most joyous and colorful feast day and usually falls from one to five weeks after western Easter. Russian Orthodox priests may marry, unlike Catholic priests.

Russian Orthodox churches can be quite striking in the American landscape; they are usually topped by one or several gleaming golden domes. Inside, the altar is separated from the congregation by a tall screen (called an *iconostasis*) that bears several paintings (called *icons*) of saints. Because the Orthodox believe that God should be praised only with the human voice, Russian churches do not have organs. Some of the most traditional churches even lack pews, leaving the worshipers to stand. Services once said in Church Slavonic, a medieval scriptural language, in recent years have mostly been said in English.

The first center of Orthodox activity in America was Alaska, but soon after the territory was sold in 1867 church headquarters moved to San Francisco, home to

Some of the color of Russian Orthodoxy's vestments and icons is shown as celebrants emerge from the sanctuary at this 1909 ceremony to bless the new bells at St. Mary's Church in Minneapolis. Orthodox immigrants proved that their faith would not die in exile.

a number of Orthodox believers. Membership in the church grew, in particular among immigrants in the industrial Northeast. The vast majority of the new members were East Slavic immigrant converts from the Greek Catholic, or Uniate, church, which follows Eastern Orthodox rites but accepts the authority of the Roman Catholic pope. By World War I, the Russian Orthodox Greek Catholic Church of America, as it was then called, had 25,000 new members. To tend to this unexpected growth, the seat of the church was transferred to the new St. Nicholas Cathedral Church in New York City; a seminary was set up first in Minneapolis, Minnesota, and then in Tenafly, New Jersey; and a monastery, St. Tikhon's, was founded near Scranton, Pennsylvania. All this occurred in the first decade of the 20th century, when the czarist government in St. Petersburg provided aid for the missionary activities of the growing church in America.

The Russian Revolution deeply affected the Russian Orthodox church at home and in the United States. The new Soviet government rejected religion, confiscating church property and wealth, closing churches, and arresting priests. Thousands of Russian Orthodox officials and worshipers fled abroad, many to the United States.

Because of disruptions and reorganization in the homeland, the Orthodox church in America was left to govern itself. Its members broke up into three jurisdictions, each fighting bitterly for control of the faithful and of church property and even taking their case to the Supreme Court. Not until the 1960s did the situation settle down, and now the Orthodox Church in America, the largest, has about 200,000 active members. The two other bodies—the Russian Orthodox Patriarchal Exarchate of Moscow and the staunchly traditional Russian Orthodox Church Outside Russia— have a total of about 60,000 members. Most of today's Orthodox believers in America (and particularly those of the latter church) were highly suspicious of the "godless" Soviet Union's role in overseeing the homeland church. With the downfall of the Soviet Union, Orthodoxy is again flourishing openly in Russia, and connections are being established between churches and congregations in the two countries.

Canadians from Russia

Of the 50,000 Canadians who claim Russian descent, more than half are religious sectarians. A prominent group among these are the Dukhobors, a sect of radical dissenters from Russian Orthodoxy who were the first Russians to emigrate to Canada in significant numbers. Persecuted for heresy and pacifism from the 18th century onward, the Dukhobors (meaning "spirit wrestlers," an epithet coined by their enemies) rejected church liturgy and held that God dwells in each person, not in a church. They also rejected secular law and preached pacifism. The Molokans in the United States actually derive from the Dukhobors, and both groups are still formally called Spiritual Christians.

The czarist government twice banished the Dukhobors to the empire's frontiers: to the Crimea in 1802 and to the Caucasus in the 1840s. The novelist Leo Tolstoy used his influence to allow them to emigrate and provided financial aid that helped about 7,500 Dukhobors to resettle in Canada in 1898–99. (On the eve of World War II, his daughter Alexandra revived his philanthropic interests and started the Tolstoy Foundation, which has assisted 30,000 Russians in coming to North America.) They settled on the prairie in Saskatchewan, where their communal living caused conflict with local officials. In 1908 their leader, Peter Verigin (1859–1924), led 6,000 Dukhobors west to set up a commune in British Columbia, but even there they clashed with the authorities over their demand to educate their children at home. By the 1960s, the dispute was resolved, with the children attending public schools in which Russian is taught a half-hour each day. Today, approximately 30,000 Dukhobors live in Canada, the vast majority of them in British Columbia, and about

About 7,500 Dukhobors from Russia, members of a sect of religious dissidents, fled their native land for the Canadian prairie in 1898–99. Today about 30,000 of their descendants live in Canada, mainly in British Columbia.

half actively practice their religion, maintain their culture, and speak Russian.

Other Russian immigrants settled in Canada in smaller numbers, having fled the revolution and civil war. During the 1920s, the Canadian government gave preference to immigrants who were farm laborers, loggers, and miners. Several hundred Russians accepted those jobs, beginning afresh in the prairie and western provinces. A new wave of displaced persons arrived in Canada from 1948 to 1953. Because of their generally higher educational level and their urban background, they settled mostly in the urban centers of southern Ontario. By the early 1970s, immigration from Russia had fallen to a few hundred persons a year, but it has picked up since with the coming of thousands of Soviet Jews. After British Columbia and Ontario, the largest number of Russian-descended citizens live in Alberta and Saskatchewan.

The very diversity of those who came to the New World from the Russian empire—religious sectarians, peasants, the upper crust—bespoke the vastness of Russia itself. Yet by the thousands these immigrants would be caught up in the new battles of an expanding continent, and the energies they expended in the workplace, at worship, and in the public limelight would test the resilience of their Russian ethnicity. 🖎

Russian immigrant iron workers at the Erie City (Pennsylvania) Iron Works meet for an Americanization class after their shift, in about 1910.

ADJUSTMENTS FOR ALL

The story of Russians in America is one of adjustment, but one with a twist. All immigrants have to make certain adjustments—they must learn a new language; they must get along with their fellow countrymen who have been in the New World for longer or shorter periods of time and have had differing experiences; they must be sensitive to the differences between first generation immigrants and their American-born descendants. Some Russian Americans faced a unique additional difficulty: the often hostile rivalry between the United States and the Soviet Union.

Though many Americans have sympathized with immigrant groups fleeing Soviet domination—such as Jews, Ukrainians, and Lithuanians—ethnic Russian immigrants have often been seen as part of the dominant, and therefore oppressor, group. Their association (direct or indirect) with either the czarist or later the Soviet rulers has often strained the immigrants' relationships with other Eastern Europeans living in the New World. It has also complicated their adaptation to American society in general.

Starting from the Bottom

For many who had skills but did not yet know English, rugged manual labor was the only work to be had. The Russian immigrants who arrived before World War I were no exception, finding employment mainly on the bottom rung of the economic ladder. The ethnic Russians either worked alongside East Slavs or joined the Russian Jews in the sweatshops of New York City's garment industry, as seamstresses, tailors, dressmakers, cutters, and in other jobs. Many of the East Slavs from the Austro-Hungarian Empire (who at the time were designated "Russian") worked as coal miners in eastern Pennsylvania or as laborers in Pittsburgh steel mills.

In Homestead, Pennsylvania, near Pittsburgh, immigrants established boardinghouses that catered to Russian-American mill workers. In such a hostelry, the immigrant could speak his mother tongue and get an occasional meal prepared in the fashion of the old country. This kind of establishment was one reason to stick with one's own ethnic group. For many immigrants, though, who were scattered in unskilled and often extremely unpleasant jobs in the factories, slaughterhouses, and meat-packing plants of New York, New Jersey, and Illinois, ethnic identity could disappear into the smoke of the factory town.

The Rise of the Working Class

We have little idea today what it was like to work in some of the factories, mines, and shops of the era from 1875 to 1920. The casualty rate among miners approached 1 in 10 yearly, and the injuries sustained by working in ill-lit rooms around unprotected machinery left thousands forever disabled. Unemployment insurance did not exist, and wages were rarely high enough to permit savings. Not many laborers complained in the early years of the Industrial Revolution, being either afraid or too tired to fight. However, some did protest by joining the increasing number of industrial strikes

Between 1880 and 1914, when poverty was widespread in the western provinces of the Russian empire and in neighboring Austria-Hungary, many immigrants found employment in the coal mines of eastern Pennsylvania.

in the last decades of the 19th century. By the 1890s, still more workers were speaking up, and by the 1910s the tales were shocking the world and galvanizing public opinion. Here is how one Russian laborer in America described his week:

> Time on the job, 91 hours; eating, about 9; street car (45 minutes each way), 10.5; sleep (7-1/2 hours a day), 52.5; dressing, undressing, washing, and so forth, 5; that totals 168 or every single hour in the week, and it's how I slave.

The 91 hours at work averages to 13 hours per day, but in fact the more common arrangement for a mill worker or coal miner was a succession of 10 or 12 hour days with a once-weekly stint of 16 or 18 hours when the shifts changed. There were even reports of workers on duty for 24 straight hours.

Despite the poor working and living conditions, American wages were relatively attractive compared to the misery many workers had left behind. The worker's dream, in America, was that everything seemed possible if you worked hard enough.

With the rise of the labor movement, the lot of these poor workers improved. Russian immigrants were prominent among the thousands who joined unions, participated in labor strikes, and fought for fairer pay and better working conditions. They often had their own Russian union branches and, along with Russian Jews, they began to play a prominent role in the leftist and socialist movements. These activities and the publication of Russian-language socialist newspapers—*Znamia*, meaning *The Banner* (1889–92), and *Progress* (1893–94)—earned the group a reputation for radical, anticapitalist politics. The reputation was sometimes deserved and sometimes not; many people caught up in the cause for better pay and working conditions were not necessarily socialists.

Outraged by poor wages and working conditions in the United States, industrial laborers took to the streets in protest. Many immigrants from Russia helped lead the effort to organize labor unions early in this century.

Once the label of "leftist" was given to Russian laborers, though, the entire group was stuck with it. The reputation had dire consequences for them after the Russian Revolution, when a "red scare" swept America in 1919 and 1920. Afraid that Bolshevism would spread first to Europe and then to America, the U.S. government cracked down on the political and labor-union activities of Russian Americans. In New York alone, police arrested 5,000 people during raids on the New York City headquarters of the Union of Russian Workers (November 1919) and the American Communist party (January 1920). Because Russians were the chief target of suspicion, the U.S. government sent 90 percent of the several thousand deportees back to the Soviet Union, although not all of them were actually Russians.

In 1920, popular opinion held that Russians were socialists, anarchists, or communists—in short, dangerously "un-American." In response to such accusations many Russian Americans tried to blend into the American mainstream by changing their religion to Protestantism and by Americanizing their names. In the process, they blurred their ethnic identity, perhaps hiding it even from themselves.

Differences Within the Community

While pre-1914 Russian immigrants were experiencing hardship and discrimination, what most historians consider the first wave of ethnic Russian immigration arrived. Refugees from Bolshevik Russia and opposed to communist rule, these "White" Russians were generally welcomed by Americans. Some one-time czarist generals and aristocrats allegedly became taxi drivers—inspiring romantic characterizations by later writers and historians—but most of this wave did not have to make such drastic changes in their new lives. The majority were highly trained professionals from the well-to-do classes of czarist society, and most of them found skilled jobs in such fields as medicine and teaching.

They also got help from American philanthropists and Russian-American fraternal, military, and educational organizations. In turn, the newcomers established new philanthropies or enhanced old ones. Among these groups were the Russian Brotherhood Society, dating back to 1900; the Russian Consolidated Mutual Aid Society, created in 1926, which founded a farm in New Jersey bearing its name; and the Tolstoy Foundation, begun in 1939.

Although this first wave of Russian immigrants adapted well to American society, they had difficulty getting along with their countrymen from the pre-1914 group, who were predominantly of the working class. The better-educated newcomers often took over the leadership of the local church and secular organizations. Older immigrants generally resented the condescending or "aristocratic" attitudes of the new immigrants. For their part, many of the refugees from the civil war wanted passionately to overthrow the Bolsheviks in Moscow and did not understand how second-generation Russian-American workers could be concerned only with getting on with their own lives.

Old Traditions in a New Land

Besides Russian Orthodoxy, perhaps the most distinctive aspect of cultural activity of Russians of any gen-

eration was and still is the Russian-American press. Its first newspaper, the *Alaska Herald-Svoboda*, was launched in San Francisco in 1868. Although it lasted only eight years, this bilingual paper was followed by many Russian-language newspapers, some of which lasted for several decades. Most were published in the eastern United States, particularly in New York City.

The Russian-language press peaked in the 1920s, when 3 daily newspapers—2 in New York and 1 in Chicago—boasted a combined daily circulation of 75,000. Of course, these were only a few of the hundreds of Russian-American newspapers and journals that represented the different political, religious, and cultural activities of the several waves of Russian immigrants. Only one major Russian-American daily newspaper survives: New York's *Novoe russkoe slovo* (*New Russian Word*), published since 1910 and therefore "the world's oldest Russian newspaper." Its circulation in the 1980s was about 43,000 copies, serving primarily the immigrants who began arriving in the 1970s. Russian-language readers are still served on the West Coast by *Russkaia zhizn'* (*Russian Life*), founded

A picnic of Russian emigrés in the 1920s. The better-off immigrants sometimes clashed with the working-class Russians who arrived before 1914.

in San Francisco in 1921, and in Canada by *Vestnik* (*Herald*), which began to appear in Toronto in 1941.

The Russian-American press gained importance by acting as a kind of mortar to hold the geographically dispersed Russian-American community together. The Russian-language papers offered a comforting familiarity in a seemingly alien environment. They also served practical functions, such as announcing religious, social, and cultural events within the Russian-American community and providing information to help the immigrants adjust to their new environment. Letters to the editor allowed readers to vent their complaints and frustrations, provoking discussion and shaping opinions within the community.

But the press has also been a propaganda instrument at times. For example, some of the first radical and socialist newspapers to circulate in the United States were printed in Russian. Among the most famous of these was *Novyi mir* (*The New World*), distributed in New York from 1916 to 1920. This newspaper had on its staff two political emigrés who were later among Bolshevik Russia's leading figures—Nikolai Bukharin (1888–1938) and Leon Trotsky (1879–1940).

The Second Wave: Prisoners of Their Past

Political events of the 1940s combined with World War II to displace millions of Europeans from their homes, many of whom left Europe entirely. This second wave, composed mainly of the displaced persons, lasted from 1945 until 1952 and brought about 50,000 Russians to the United States. Most did not come directly from the Soviet Union but via many divergent paths. Some had been deported to Nazi Germany during the war; others had fled westward to escape the advancing Soviet Red Army in 1944 and 1945; and still others were "White" (anti-Bolshevik) Russians who in the 1920s had settled in European countries that came under Soviet domination after World War II. These countries included Czechoslovakia, Yugoslavia, Poland, and the Baltic states of Latvia, Lithuania, and Estonia. Some even came from China (especially Harbin), where they had settled after the Russian Revolution, only to be uprooted once again after mainland China became communist in 1949.

Unlike the postrevolution wave of aristocrats and professionals, this second wave included Russians from all classes, particularly farm laborers and industrial workers. But a few were well-known emigrés who had lived in western Europe since the 1920s. The most famous was Alexander Kerensky (1881–1970), the liberal politician and head of the postczarist Provisional Government overthrown by the Bolsheviks. After spending the war years in France, Kerensky arrived in New York City in 1940, where he stayed for the rest of his life, lecturing and writing about the momentous events of 1917, which he had tried—in vain—to shape.

The Russians who came to America during this second wave faced a difficult adjustment, though they related well to the aristocratic, better-educated first wave. The difficulty began before they even set foot on American soil, and, once again, Soviet-American relations were the source of the problem.

The war against Nazi Germany had put the United States and Soviet Union on the same side as military allies. When the Nazis and Japanese surrendered in 1945, the Allies were obliged to live up to the various agreements that they had made among themselves during wartime. One such agreement declared that the western powers, including the United States and Great Britain, would repatriate (send back) all persons living in Western Europe who had been born in Soviet territory—by force, if necessary.

At first, U.S. military authorities in Europe cooperated in the repatriation program. Between 1945 and 1948, 2 million Russian refugees were returned to the Soviet Union. There they met with exactly what they had feared: Many were imprisoned, exiled within the USSR (to Siberia, for example), or even executed. To escape repatriation, the Russians who remained in Eu-

Thousands of Russians who fled west from the Bolsheviks in the 1920s and then fled the Nazis during World War II were admitted to the United States between 1945 and 1955. These displaced persons constituted the second wave of Russian emigration.

rope claimed they belonged to different Slavic nationalities—anything but Russian.

After the war the Soviet government, led by Joseph Stalin, imposed its rule on Eastern Europe and announced its intention to spread communism throughout the world. In America there was widespread suspicion that Soviet agents and spies had infiltrated the Russians who escaped repatriation and immigrated to the United States. And indeed, some of these agents may have joined the second wave of Russian immigrants who came to Canada and the United States. A few immigrants, spies possibly among them, found jobs as university professors, government translators, and in other potentially influential posts.

The threat to democracy was never great, but at this point anti-Soviet feelings ran wild in some quarters. A second red scare, like the one of 1919–20, seized the land, spearheaded by Senator Joseph McCarthy of Wisconsin. Congressional investigations into communist infiltration went on throughout the early 1950s, and many people were wrongly accused of communist activity or sympathies. Those accused were blacklisted and often lost their jobs. (The persecution that accompanied this red scare came to be called McCarthyism.) One result was that many of the recent Russian immigrants felt compelled to maintain a low ethnic profile. Whether in Europe or North America, it was not a good time for a person to admit Russian ancestry.

Senator Joseph McCarthy of Wisconsin (left) led a government inquiry of suspected communist sympathizers in the early 1950s. Thousands of Americans were accused and many Russian Americans felt compelled to conceal their ancestry.

The Emigration Door Closes

After the establishment of Soviet rule, strict controls made emigration difficult at times. And when controls were clamped on, families could be divided—many of those who left with the hope of smoothing the way for their families found instead that the border had closed up behind them. Some left unsuspecting and were trapped abroad. One 16-year-old girl proudly sailed to America as the family's representative at her immigrant brother's wedding. She dreamily planned her return to Odessa, anticipating the tales she would tell. But it was 1917. Return became impossible, and relatives were suddenly untraceable. She would never know whether, as she suspected, her family had arranged the trip so she could escape the coming revolution, or even whether they had survived.

That story was repeated a thousand times during the years of Soviet rule. In the 1980s, however, the situation improved markedly for those Russians wishing to leave and for emigrés who wanted to return home to visit family and friends. The next chapter will look at some beneficiaries of the relaxed rules, the third wave who have revitalized Russian culture in the New World and given it their own generation's stamp. ✍

Christian and Jew, rich and poor, citizens of Russia and the Soviet Union managed to emigrate to the West despite the whims of history and an adverse political climate. These Old Believers arrived in 1963.

Since 1970, tens of thousands of third-wave Russian immigrants, most of them Jewish, have settled in and revived the Brighton Beach section of Brooklyn, New York.

A GENERATION REMOVED

I t has seldom been easy to leave Russia or the Soviet Union. For most of the nation's history, official policy has strongly deterred emigration, either out of the leaders' fear that too much Western influence on the people could lead to trouble, or out of the simple belief that Russians belong in Mother Russia. Yet in times of war, great economic upheaval, or social deprivation, thousands managed to leave the country to start new lives in North America.

Recent twists of fate have helped Russians wishing to emigrate. In the détente of the early 1970s, the Soviets agreed to begin allowing as many as 250,000 citizens to emigrate. In theory, only Jews and Armenians "seeking to reunite" with family members could leave. In practice, many others left—political dissidents, scientists, writers and artists, and human-rights activists whom the Soviets classified as "undesirables."

Some Soviet citizens who were not Jewish had "Jew" stamped on their passports because Jews had a better chance of receiving permission to leave. A number of the emigrants, though, really were Russian Jews. Unlike the earlier waves of Jewish emigrants, many of whom spoke Yiddish as their native language and came from Eastern Europe, the Russian Jews of the recent immigration speak Russian and are culturally Russian. Many of them lived in Moscow and other Russian cities and are less strongly connected to Judaism than the earlier Jewish immigrants.

A significant number of people who have arrived in this third wave of immigration have settled in metropolitan New York; others have headed for southern California. They have transformed some districts, such as Brooklyn's Brighton Beach and part of Los Angeles, into vibrant ethnic neighborhoods. Others have fanned out across the U.S. and Canadian landscape.

The Arduous Path to the West

The third wave of Russian immigrants has attracted attention for several reasons. Though we often think of the period from 1880 to 1914 as the years of America's greatest immigration, since 1956 just as many newcomers from around the world have added themselves to the population of the United States and Canada. This new immigration boom includes, since 1970, about 150,000 people from the Soviet Union or Russia.

Their path to these shores has been a different one from that of their predecessors. Those who were forced to leave Russia before its revolution or during World War II usually made intermediary stops in Europe, the Middle East, or the Far East, finally arriving by boat in the New World after some months or years in limbo. The third wave, on the other hand, comes by airplane, and in most cases directly from Moscow with a brief layover in Vienna or Rome. What hardship they suffer along the way is mainly of the bureaucratic sort: waiting in long lines in Moscow or some provincial capital for a visa and travel documents.

Some older Russian immigrants think the third wave has had it easy, with no revolution, war, murderous Cossacks, or Nazis to block their way. But modern emigration procedures have been grim in their own way. A Soviet citizen who wished to leave almost always lost his or her job after applying for an exit visa; the family might have lost its apartment as well. Most applicants waited six months or longer to learn whether they would receive permission to emigrate. Some waited for years. Though the emigrants of the third wave were not shot at like those of an earlier time, the preparation for boarding a plane to the West was often as laborious and bankrupting, psychologically and financially, as boarding a ship before 1950. Emigration procedures have become easier and faster—although no less costly—in post-USSR Russia.

Settling In

A Russian emigrant who settles in the Brighton Beach neighborhood of Brooklyn finds a mixture of old and new. Between 15,000 and 25,000 Russian speakers populate the district (estimates are difficult because the emigrés' past has taught them to be suspicious of government tabulators), which in previous decades was home to Italians, Jews, and Irish, and still bears traces of their presence. Yet Russian is spoken on the streets, and in many stores along Brighton Beach Avenue or Ocean Parkway a shopper can get by in no other language. The neighborhood has gained the epithet "Odessa by the Sea," in reference to the southern Soviet city from which many of the emigrés come. The area's representative to the U.S. Congress, Stephen Solarz, has printed a "Special Washington Report" newsletter in Russian for the residents, though many are not yet U.S. citizens.

The solicitous attention of government officials and a linguistic bond do not make the process of settling in perfectly smooth, however. The best recent book on the Soviet emigrés, *Moscow to Main Street* by Victor Ripp, details some of the obstacles to integration—the language, for one. A great number of the emigrés, just like their counterparts in Paris in the 1920s, start off as cabdrivers, warehouse workers, or translators, regardless of previous education or work experience.

U.S. Congressman Stephen Solarz, whose district includes Brighton Beach, has issued a newsletter printed in Cyrillic script to reach his Russian-speaking constituency.

Ripp's book investigates many emigrants' deep ambivalence about giving up their past. The strain of nationalism that runs through Russian citizens, especially those who survived the Nazi onslaught, is deeper than most non-Russians can imagine. Even those, including Russian Jews, who were ill-treated by the Soviet regime feel a reverent attachment to their homeland. To criticize Russia's leaders is a way of life for these emigrants, but no non-Russian should dare to criticize, as national pride for the homeland might give the Russian cause to take offense. Alexander Galich, a songwriter who emigrated in 1973, summed up this paradox best when he said, "I left the Soviet Union; I did not leave Russia."

The ambivalence can also be striking in Russian-American teenagers. They wear the same clothes and listen to the same rock music as their classmates, in most cases, and in Brooklyn they can be street tough in a way Europeans generally do not need to be. Yet they speak Russian and do not take to American sports quickly, preferring soccer. One teenager whom Ripp interviewed vowed that if a Soviet Russian soccer team came to play against an American one in New York, he would always root for the Russians. His family had first come to Los Angeles, but moved to Brooklyn, where they could always speak Russian. Still, he does not call himself a Russian. When asked if he thinks of himself as a Jew, then, he replied more emphatically, "No, not that either."

This second paradox also troubles many of the recent emigrés. In the USSR their national designation

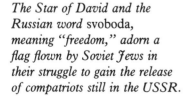

The Star of David and the Russian word svoboda, *meaning "freedom," adorn a flag flown by Soviet Jews in their struggle to gain the release of compatriots still in the USSR.*

was "Jewish," meaning they are a group the authorities do not consider Russian; yet most were not religiously observant and did not live in a republic of their own, such as Armenia or the Ukraine. Nor are many of them practicing Jews in Brooklyn, where they sometimes feel pressure to become part of the larger community of observant Jews, to renew their faith. One woman told Ripp, "In the Soviet Union we were despised for being too Jewish; here we are criticized for not being Jewish enough. *That's* the fate of a Soviet Jew, never to satisfy anyone." There are some Orthodox Russian Americans who do not believe that the Russian Jews now settling in the United States as part of the third wave of immigration merit the name "Russian."

Working and Getting Ahead

Emigrating from Russia means leaving behind many things. Parents discovered that Russian children get a better general education than Americans. As a result, many Russian children jump ahead a grade or two in American schools after they have mastered English. Also, the average Russian engineer has better general training than his or her American counterpart, yet suffers professionally upon arriving in the United States because of the greater degree of specialization in American scientific and technical work.

Because the Soviet government guaranteed a job to anyone who could work, immigrants who came to the United States during the Soviet era were ill-prepared to compete for jobs in interviews. Many immigrants begin with service jobs, such as working in restaurants or driving cabs. Others become entrepreneurs, opening their own businesses. Yet although they work hard, shopkeepers and businesspeople in Russian-American communities such as Brighton Beach have sometimes avoided joining the local board of trade or getting involved in politics because those activities reminded them of Communist party organizations.

Contrary to many immigrants' dreams, hard work does not usually make one a millionaire in the United

Nathan Schiller, a former filmmaker who was persecuted in the Soviet Union, now runs this souvenir store in Cambridge, Massachusetts. His new life is not easy, he says, "but it's better."

States, or even guarantee financial security. And the cost of housing in many American cities means that recent immigrants share homes or apartments with their older relatives or in-laws, just as they did in Russia. Still, the overall feeling about working in America, as one man said, is, "It's better, of course. But it's not paradise."

Some Who Have Made It

In contrast to some of their predecessors, third-wave immigrants are wealthier and more likely to be highly trained professionals, such as doctors, engineers, or teachers. And as a group, they seem to have adapted to American society quickly: In less than a decade many have become successful. While some may try to sustain their former cultural environment, most seem more interested in achieving economic success and fully Americanizing themselves and their children.

One who has done so is Yuri Radzievsky. After a highly successful career in Moscow as the host of a television show he describes as a cross between "College Bowl" and "Saturday Night Live," Radzievsky ran afoul of officialdom and chose to emigrate in 1973. At the age of 28, with an engineering degree, teaching experience, authorship of two technical books, and a television career behind him, he launched an advertising and translation service on a shoestring budget. It is now a multimillion-dollar marketing and communications firm, involved in adapting U.S. advertising campaigns to foreign markets or foreign products to the American market, and it is a subsidiary of the advertising giant Ogilvy & Mather.

Despite his youthful success in Moscow, Radzievsky said of his prospects there, "I could see my life in a very long tunnel . . . with very limited possibilities." He recognizes that from a materialistic point of view he has improved his and his family's lot; but he came to the West "in quest of excellence, in search of better surroundings for myself." There was also what he calls "the Jewish question." The son of a Jewish mother and a Russian father, he was classified as a Jew, leaving him

One of the most successful of the recent Russian immigrants is Yuri Radzievsky. In 1973 he left an engineering, teaching, and television career in Moscow and subsequently started his own advertising firm in New York.

vulnerable to a daily anti-Semitism in Moscow far more pronounced, in his view, than is found in America.

In Radzievsky's opinion, the third wave of Russian Americans is likely to do very well, better than those of previous generations. Their lifetime of "getting along with and around" the Soviet system has given them "a practicality of the brain . . . and more resilience" than the earlier waves had to have. "The emigrés are people who don't take things for granted," he said, and this quality may stand them in good stead as they make their way through the capitalist system.

Radzievsky's success has not swept away all his misgivings. He says with amusement tinged with wistfulness that his teenage daughter speaks English with no accent and Russian with an American accent: She is becoming thoroughly American. A more pointed source of concern is his mother, aged 70, who still lives in Moscow, unwilling to emigrate. She and other parents of those living abroad, he says, are "like an old tree which cannot be replanted in new soil. Their roots are too deep."

Radzievsky is just one success story, of which there are a growing number. Most current Russian emigrés arrive highly educated, many with the benefit of good technical training that allows them to work with electronics or computers. Others bring only the need to make money and a wish to preserve some part of their past. A case in point is the National Restaurant, in Brighton Beach, which was started from scratch by emigrés as a hideaway for street-weary refugees. It now serves an average of 3,000 diners every weekend, and the grocery store attached to it is a major enterprise, also drawing people from all sectors of New York's diverse population. The National's popularity is also a sign of the steadily improving relations between Soviet emigrés and the American public at large.

The members of the third wave are, in their own way, as diverse as the generations that preceded them in crossing the Atlantic. Among them are hard-edged political dissidents from the Soviet control apparatus; others who merely had the bad luck to be overheard complaining; those frustrated into emigrating by the harassment of the KGB (the Soviet secret police); and seekers of religious freedom, such as the 1,000 Bukharan Jews from Tadzhikistan in central Asia, who still speak Tadzhi while living in the Borough Park section of Brooklyn, surrounded by speakers of Yiddish, or in Cincinnati, Ohio. The third wave also includes many entertainers such as the comedian Yaakov Smirnoff, who has appeared in various television spots.

The third wave also brought a group of Russian artists to the United States. Many settled in the Soho district of Manhattan, elsewhere in New York City, or in neighboring Jersey City, New Jersey. Some of them had left the Soviet Union "to paint the way we want to." Among the more prominent are Mikhail Chemiakin, Lev Meshberg, Oleg Tselkov, and the successful pair who create paintings together, Vitaly Komar (1943–) and Alexander Melamid (1945–). Komar and Melamid have attempted to bridge the culture gap by creating in a style that combines American Pop art and Soviet socialist realism. This means they often project Soviet political slogans onto typically American images, as in their 1980 canvas, "Onward to the Final Victory of Capitalism," a twist on a Soviet exhortation to workers to strive for socialism.

It is ironic that at home Komar and Melamid were labeled dissidents because they did "American art," for in New York they are acutely aware of their Russianness. "We wanted to be Americans but realized we couldn't," Melamid said. "Part of our past, for example the Stalinist period, belongs to everybody." When asked to explain just exactly what this meant, he replied that Joseph Stalin is not viewed by most people in the USSR as a tyrant: "I was eight when Stalin died, Vitaly ten. For children Stalin was a figure of love and protection. For our parents he was terrifying, not for us."

Having received far more classical artistic training than most American artists ever receive, Komar and Melamid are able to blend their New World perceptions with their Old World education. The result is a depth, irony, and humor in their paintings and assemblages that bespeak multiple cultural influences, a drama that is more evident as they absorb each passing year in New York. One piece displayed in 1988 at the Guggenheim Museum in New York combined elements of a fabulistic archaeological dig with a glowing newspaper account of the dig; the point is that modern-day sculptors can excavate our past just as surely as scientists do; and that the press can easily shape our opinions. They keep in touch with life on the street, too, having developed a taste for stoop culture—walking around, observing people observing them from the stoops of their buildings.

Leaving a staid old culture for an alluring yet all-consuming new one creates tension in an emigré that can make him or her feel forever out of place. An axiom of long standing says that Russia has its head in Europe and its body in Asia. For many of the newest Russian Americans, the axiom is turned 90 degress: Their hearts may be in Russia, but their bodies are in America. ❧

The duo of Vitaly Komar (standing) and Alexander Melamid have brought a new perspective to the American art scene.

In 1941 Igor Sikorsky acted as his own test pilot in the helicopter he invented. He also made important innovations in airplane design.

RUSSIAN CULTURE, AMERICAN LIFE

You can be a citizen anywhere, but my soul
will always be a Russian one.
—Mikhail Baryshnikov

Like most other peoples from Europe, some Russian immigrants and, in particular, their descendants have severed all ties with the culture of their ancestral homeland and have been assimilated into American society. Most, however, have adapted without entirely abandoning their native culture. And as public acceptance and knowledge of things Russian expands, Russian Americans may feel even freer to show pride in their ancestry.

The following second- and third-wave immigrants from Russia—some ethnic Russians, others Russian Jews—have made enormous contributions in many fields. They have applied the greatness of Russian tradition to the opportunities for expression offered in America, enriching both cultures.

Science and Scholarship

The name Igor Sikorsky (1889–1972) is linked forever with the history of aviation. While studying at the Imperial Naval College of St. Petersburg and the Mechanical College of the Polytechnic Institute in Kiev, Sikorsky learned everything he could about the 1903 flight of the Wright brothers. After finishing school in

1908, Sikorsky went to France to study its new aircraft industry. Even in these early years of aviation history, he was fascinated by the idea of building a helicopter. And although he attempted to build one when he returned to Russia, he was more successful with conventional winged aircraft.

In 1913 Sikorsky constructed the world's first multi-motored plane—a four-motored airplane for which the czar awarded him a medal. Bomber versions of this airplane were used by the Russian army in World War I. After the Russian Revolution, Sikorsky's aircraft business failed and he emigrated, first to western Europe, then to New York in 1919. After teaching fellow immigrants in a Russian-language college in New York City, Sikorsky raised enough money to establish the Sikorsky Aviation Corporation in Bridgeport, Connecticut, in 1923. (In 1929 his company was bought by a larger aircraft firm, and it is now a division of the United Technologies Corporation.)

During the 1920s, Sikorsky designed a succession of new airplanes, including the famous S-38 10-seater for Pan American Airways, and later the S-42, which was used for the first regular flights across the Atlantic and Pacific. But his dream of building a helicopter never faded, and in 1939, after much experimentation, he built the world's first. This model was used by the U.S. Army during World War II.

In addition to his contribution to aviation, Sikorsky was active in the Russian community in the United States. He was instrumental in building the Russian Orthodox church in Bridgeport, and he also wrote two religious and philosophical books, *The Message of the Lord's Prayer* (1942) and *The Invisible Encounter* (1947).

Many other distinguished Russian scientists and scholars entered the leading ranks of American industry and scholarship as well. Among the best known are George Gamow (1904–68), the nuclear physicist and popularizer of the "big bang" theory of the origin of the universe; George Kistiakowsky (1900–83), a chemist and presidential adviser on science; Wassily Leontieff (1906–), the Nobel Prize–winning economist who formulated the influential input-output system of economic analysis; Alexander Petrunkevitch (1875–1964), the author of numerous works in the field of zoology; and Vladimir Zworykin (1889–1982), the physicist and electronic engineer known as the "father of television." In Canada, among the most prominent of the Russian emigrants have been the four sons of Count Paul Ignatieff, who was the last minister of education under Czar Nicholas II. The four—Nicholas, Vladimir, Alexis, and George—were active in both engineering and government.

Other Russian scholars have enriched America's knowledge of their native land. In fact, much of America's present understanding of Russia and the Soviet Union comes from the work of immigrants such as theologian Georges Florovsky (1893–1979), literary critic Gleb Struve (1898–1985), and historians Michael Rostovtsev (1870–1972), Michael Florinsky (1894–1981), Michael Karpovich (1888–1959), Alexander Vasiliev (1867–1953), and George Vernadsky (1887–1973). Still making names for themselves are the hundreds of scholars and critics, many now in their prime, who have arrived in the West in the last decade.

In the Arts

The long and spirited legacy of Russian cultural life has been served well by Russian Americans in the arts. Some, especially writers, musicians, and dancers, contribute to the ongoing creation of modern Russian culture. Because of political and intellectual controls in the Soviet Union, two distinct schools of the Russian arts developed through the 1980s: the Soviet Russian variety, which for all its various strengths did not have much contact with the rest of the world, and Russian emigré culture, which offered the best of both worlds.

Since World War II, New York City has become a world center of Russian emigré literature. The Russica, Possev, and newer Bukinist publishing houses specialize in Russian-language literature, as does the journal of Russian literature, culture, and politics *Novyi zhurnal* (*The New Journal*), founded in New York in 1942.

To read Russian emigré literature is to gain insight into Russian-American thought and emotion and how these emigrés have or have not adjusted to their new home. In general, three themes have dominated this literature: a love for the homeland, "Mother Russia"; the difficulty of adjusting to life in foreign countries; and the problem of loneliness. One poet, Iurii Ivask (1910–), probably summed up best what seems to be a universal feeling among Russian Americans when he asked, "Who can be as alone as an emigrant?"

Since the first wave of immigration after World War I, several Russian writers have continued to publish in

An exemplar of independent womanhood as well as a great sculptor, Louise Nevelson gave new theoretical value to wood, boxes, shadow, and light.

their native language in the United States. Among the more successful and popular from that generation are the poets Ivask and Igor Chinnov (1911–) and prose writers Rodion Berezov (1896–) and Vasily Yanovsky (1906–). Russian-American literature has been enriched in the past two decades with the establishment of new literary journals and the arrival of new writers such as the novelists Vasily Aksyonov (1932–), Edward Limonov (1944–), and Vladimir Voinivich (1932–).

New York has also become a center for Russian emigré artists. One of the most renowned was Louise Nevelson (née Berliawsky, 1899–1988), born in Kiev to a family of Jewish lumber merchants who moved to Maine in 1902. She studied in Berlin, Paris, and Vienna, finally settling in New York. There she slowly developed a style of sculpture that employed boxes and scraps of wood found on the street to depict imaginary cityscapes and surreal environments. The shadows created by the bits of wood can give her assemblages the texture of a forest, or something else—a critic in the *New York Times*, commenting on a black wall sculpture, was reminded of "something not easily found in North America: the impact of carved wood and stone in a twilit Gothic cathedral." Nevelson did not gain much recognition until she was in her fifties, but now there are examples of her work in parks, museums, and public spaces across the United States.

Vladimir Nabokov was at home writing in Russian or in English. His most widely read novel, Lolita, *describes a European man's infatuation with an adolescent American girl.*

Writers

Of the Russians who have written in English, Vladimir Nabokov (1899–1977) is perhaps the most celebrated. Born into an aristocratic St. Petersburg household, he and his family were forced to flee from the revolution in 1917. He lived for periods in Berlin, Paris, and Cambridge, England, before coming to the United States in 1940. He began then to write in English, and to translate many Russian works, both his own and others'— his English rendition of Alexander Pushkin's novel in

A proponent of Russian Orthodox religious tradition, a scourge of the USSR's prison-camp system, and a critic of America's supposed moral weakness and commercialism, Alexander Solzhenitsyn has sealed his reputation as one of the world's most important writers.

verse, *Eugene Onegin*, is one of the finest. Nabokov's facility with language is evident both in the breadth of his writing and in the wordplay he employed.

The most widely read of his many novels is *Lolita* (1958), the story of a middle-aged European man who falls in love with a spoiled 12-year-old American girl. Controversy over the subject matter and, later, the motion picture based on his novel made Nabokov's story particularly well known. The lectures on Russian, British, French, and German literature he gave while teaching at Cornell and Harvard universities, and his lectures on Cervantes' masterpiece *Don Quixote*, all show Nabokov's tremendous erudition and his cosmopolitan turn of mind.

In a lighter vein, the novel *Pnin* (1957) tells how a Russian-emigré professor at a bucolic American college struggles with the new language and customs of his adopted land. When he proudly announces that within two or three years none of the students will know he is a Russian, all of his friends burst out laughing. Nabokov was also one of the world's leading lepidopterists (butterfly experts). And his memoir *Speak, Memory* (1966) gives a charming account of life among the wealthy in czarist Russia.

One of the most renowned Russian Americans living today is Alexander Solzhenitsyn (1918–), an outspoken dissident writer who had once been imprisoned in the Soviet Union for his views. He was born in Kislovodsk, a health resort in the foothills of the northern Caucasus Mountains. After graduating with degrees in mathematics and physics in 1941, he served as an artillery commander in the Red Army during World War II. His trouble with Soviet authorities began in the last year of the war when he wrote a letter criticizing Soviet leader Joseph Stalin. He was arrested in February 1945 and sentenced to eight years in a Soviet labor camp. While in prison he began to write, continuing to do so after his release in 1953 and his return from internal exile three years later.

Solzhenitsyn catapulted to fame in 1962 when his short novel about prison-camp life, *One Day in the Life of Ivan Denisovich*, was published. Two English translations of the work soon appeared, making him a public figure in the Western world. However, after the Soviet change of leadership in 1964, Solzhenitsyn was increasingly criticized by the authorities and was unable to get his other novels published. These included *The Cancer Ward*, *The First Circle*, *August 1914*, and the nonfiction work *The Gulag Archipelago*. Eventually, all of these books were published abroad.

Solzhenitsyn's realistic depiction of life in the Soviet Union and his outspoken criticism of official cultural and political policies enhanced his reputation abroad. In 1970 he was awarded in absentia the Nobel Prize in literature. But his anti-Soviet activity soon resulted in his arrest and deportation to Switzerland in 1974, from where he emigrated to the United States. Unlike most of his fellow intellectuals in the third wave, Solzhenitsyn lives comfortably on his earnings as a writer. He even provides financial support for Russian-language publishing ventures in the West as well as for the families of dissidents still living in the Soviet Union. A major biography of him appeared in 1984.

From his involuntary exile abroad, Solzhenitsyn continues to speak out against the evils of modern civilization. Now living in semiseclusion in Vermont, he writes criticism of both the Soviet regime and the

Poet Irina Ratushinskaya was released from a Soviet prison camp in 1986, where she served time for propounding human rights and for writing poetry the authorities said caused "agitation." She now lives in Illinois.

Joseph Brodsky, an American resident since 1972, won the Nobel Prize in literature in 1987 for his stirring essays and poetry about Russian culture and Soviet life.

West—especially the United States, for what he perceives to be its moral weakness and naïveté in dealing with the Soviets. He argues that Russia's future depends on moral regeneration and a revival of religious principles based on traditional Russian Orthodoxy.

Irina Ratushinskaya (1954–) is another of the recently arrived political dissident writers. As a poet in the Soviet Union, she came under increasing pressure from the authorities for her writing and her human-rights activity and in 1983 was sentenced to seven years of hard labor in a prison camp, to be followed by five years of internal exile. Denied paper or pen while in the camp, she kept at her craft by an ingenious method: She etched words of poetry into a bar of soap with a sharpened match, memorized them, then wrote more; she recited poems to herself all day to cement them in her memory. She was unexpectedly freed in 1986, on the eve of the Reagan-Gorbachev summit in Iceland, and allowed to go to England for medical help. She now teaches at Northwestern University in Evanston, Illinois, continuing with poetry and writing about the maltreatment of women in the Soviet camps. Her first book of poems to appear in English was *Beyond the Limit* (1987).

Joseph Brodsky (1940–) was awarded the Nobel Prize in literature in 1987 for a life's work that had already marked him as one of the century's great poets. An American resident since 1972, he drew a sentence of five years (later commuted to two) in the Soviet Union for "parasitism" when his work did not meet with official approval. In his books of poems, *Selected Poems* (1974), *A Part of Speech* (1980), and *To Urania* (1988), and in the essay collection *Less Than One* (1986), he shows himself to be aghast at what control the modern totalitarian state can wield over a person's life and imagination. As one who lives by his creative powers, Brodsky is most concerned with the glories of poetic language and Western culture, and he sees the great Russian literary tradition coming to an end if the Soviet authorities do not soon begin to grant their writers much more liberty.

Though born a Jew, he grants that the Christian tradition has had a greater hand in shaping his mind, but that Buddhism, in his opinion, offers more metaphysical depth than either of the Western creeds. Dostoyevsky and the Anglo-American poet W. H. Auden have been two of the chief influences on him. He composes his poems in both Russian and English.

Brodsky represents the more worldly bent of many of the third-wave immigrants, those who would prefer to see relations between East and West mended rather than inflame them with political rhetoric. When asked how Russians have influenced American life, he said that their growing presence in the West may have yielded an "increased degree of sobriety in political relations" between the rival governments.

Music

Russian Americans have made an especially distinctive mark in the world of music. In the 19th century, the United States had already embraced Russia's greatest living composers. In fact, when New York City's Carnegie Hall opened in 1891 (designed in part by a Russian American, Vladimir Stolishnikoff), the first concert featured an all-Russian program conducted by Peter Ilyich Tchaikovsky.

At first, prominent Russian musicians came to the United States on concert tours, but after World War I many arrived to stay longer or permanently, in the process helping to change the course of 20th-century music. Igor Stravinsky (1882–1971), one of the geniuses of modern music, settled in the United States in 1929 and became a citizen six years later.

Stravinsky was born in the seaside resort of Oranienbaum on the Gulf of Finland near the Russian imperial capital of St. Petersburg. Although he was trained in law, Stravinsky's first love was music, especially that of Russia's great 19th-century composers, Glinka, Tchaikovsky, and Rimsky-Korsakov. Yet his own compositions departed radically from those of his mentors. Success first came in 1909, when he began a 20-year association with Sergei Diaghilev's troupe, Bal-

*Composer and conductor Igor Stravinsky is perhaps best known for the ballets—*The Firebird, Petroushka, *and* The Rite of Spring—*that were set to his music by Sergei Diaghilev.*

lets Russes, for which he wrote three ballets in rapid succession—*The Firebird* (1910), *Petrouchka* (1911), and *The Rite of Spring* (1913). The third contained bold orchestral instrumentation, rapidly changing rhythmic patterns, and daring harmonies, making it the focus of both critical praise and protest, and prompting scholars to conclude that modern music began with this composition.

When World War I broke out, Stravinsky was in western Europe. He did not return to Russia after the war, remaining in France where he worked on small orchestral arrangements, ballets, opera-oratorios, and concertos. In 1930 he composed *Symphony of Psalms* for the 50th anniversary of the Boston Symphony Orchestra. He toured the United States as a conductor and pianist before making it his home. He continued to write symphonies and operas, his most well known opera being *The Rake's Progress* (1951). Constant experimentation led him to the nonharmonic and nontonal serial style that marks his later compositions.

By the end of his career, Stravinsky had gained many honors. In 1962 President John F. Kennedy honored him at the White House; he was made a knight commander by Pope John XXIII; and the Composers Union of the USSR invited him to visit his native land after a 48-year absence.

Music connoisseurs regard Vladimir Horowitz (1904–) as one of the world's most dazzling pianists, and for more than 60 years critics have praised his phenomenal technique and virtuosity. Horowitz began his studies at age 6 and made his public debut after finishing at the Kiev Conservatory 11 years later. However, the Bolshevik revolution soon upset his comfortable family surroundings. During those difficult first years of Soviet rule, the prodigy supported his family by giving concerts, gaining national fame along the way.

In 1925 Horowitz was permitted to leave the Soviet Union for a "study tour" of western Europe. He never returned. After a triumphal tour of European capitals, he went to America in 1928. His first concert—at New

Vladimir Horowitz, one of the great piano virtuosos of the century, returned to his native Soviet Union for a recital in 1986. It was his first visit in more than 60 years.

York's Carnegie Hall—was a historic musical event: Horowitz electrified the audience with a performance of the *First Piano Concerto* by Tchaikovsky, the Russian composer who 37 years before had conducted at the hall's inaugural concert.

During the 1930s, Horowitz worked closely with the great conductor Arturo Toscanini, and he eventually married the maestro's daughter Wanda. By 1942 Horowitz had become the highest-paid artist in America, but he frequently interrupted his career with periods of seclusion. In 1953 he left the performing stage for 12 years, although during this absence he made several recordings, and from 1962 to 1965 he won an unprecedented four straight Grammy awards for making the best classical album of the year.

Since his most recent return to public life in 1965, Horowitz has performed with the leading orchestras. But he still feels attached to his homeland, and his wish to return was fulfilled in the spring of 1986, when he thrilled capacity crowds in Moscow and Leningrad. He said, "I have never forgotten my Russia. I remember the smells when the snow melts and the spring arrives. I had to go back to Russia before I died." Today, the Horowitz legend lives on in Russia and America.

Horowitz has at times overshadowed some of his compatriots who also have made enormous contributions in the United States. Among those who have lit up the stage are Serge Koussevitzky (1874–1951), who served as conductor of the Boston Symphony Orchestra from 1924 to 1949; Fyodor Chaliapin (1873–1938), the Metropolitan Opera's leading bass during the 1920s; the composer Alexander Gretchaninov (1864–1956); and the composer and pianist Sergei Rachmaninoff (1873–1943).

Recently arrived musicians include the cello virtuoso and conductor Mstislav Rostropovich (1927–), musical director of the National Symphony Orchestra in Washington, D.C., since 1974 and his wife, the noted soprano Galina Vishnevskaya (1927–). Her memoir *Galina* (1984) gives an eerie account of how music and musicians were subordinated to political objectives in the Soviet Union.

Dance

George Balanchine (1904–83) has been described as the "finest choreographer of our time." Born Iurii Balantchivadze of Georgian parents in St. Petersburg, he trained from 1914 to 1917 at the Imperial Ballet School. His first performance was with the Soviet State Dancers after the Russian Revolution. In 1924 he left the group during a tour in western Europe and joined the famed Ballets Russes in Paris, under the direction of Sergei Diaghilev. Diaghilev encouraged Balanchine to concentrate on choreography.

In 1933 Balanchine came to the United States. The next year, he cofounded the School of American Ballet, which became the New York City Ballet in 1948. Balanchine remained with the company until his death, creating nearly 200 ballets and training many of today's leading American ballet dancers. He found inspiration in the music of Bach, Schubert, and Mozart, but the music of 20th century composers such as Arnold Schoenberg, Anton Webern, and Charles Ives also came to life with Balanchine's choreography. Perhaps his greatest ballets were inspired by the compositions of Igor Stravinsky, his contemporary and fellow countryman. During his long and prolific career, Balanchine also choreographed 19 Broadway musicals, including

Modern dance owes much of its inspiration and form to the master choreographer George Balanchine. Up until his death in 1983, he was still improving and reshaping American ballet.

On Your Toes (1936), and 4 motion pictures. Balanchine is remembered with great affection throughout the dance world, both by the ballerinas he trained (among them the four he married), and by the new fans he drew to the dance world.

From the beginning of this century, many more of Russia's—and the world's—greatest dancers and choreographers have graced American stages. In the 1920s, such ballet immortals as Sergei Diaghilev, Anna Pavlova (1881–1931), and Michel Fokine (1880–1942) thrilled American audiences while making dance history.

The tradition of Russian ballet in America has continued with the arrival in the past two decades of several more dancers, chief among them Mikhail Baryshnikov (1948–). Baryshnikov, like Balanchine, has attracted new enthusiasts to dance with the beauty of his form. In the decade since he left the Soviet Union, Western critics have called him "technically the most gifted and the most stylish male dancer in the world today." And on July 4, 1986, he became an American citizen at the Miss Liberty Celebration in New York City.

He was born of Russian parents in Riga, the capital of the Latvian Soviet Socialist Republic. His mother encouraged him to study classical dance, and in 1966 he joined Leningrad's famed Kirov Ballet. After winning the coveted gold medal at an international ballet competition in Bulgaria, his reputation grew quickly, and several ballets were choreographed especially for him. But by the 1970s, he began to grow discontented with the Soviet Union's limited artistic horizons. In particular, he was attracted to the choreography George Balanchine was doing for the New York City Ballet company.

In 1974, while on tour in Canada, Baryshnikov defected to the West. During temporary residence in Canada, he began to perform in the United States, and he made his American debut at Lincoln Center's New York State Theater in July 1974. Here, he danced with another outstanding performer and recent defector from the Kirov Ballet, Natalia Makarova (1940–). Soon Baryshnikov settled in the United States, dancing with the American Ballet Theater and Balanchine's troupe, too. In 1980 he was named artistic director of the American Ballet Theater, a post he still holds.

Like other great dancers who came from Russia, Baryshnikov stuns audiences with his versatility and transports them to the world of classical Russian form through his movement. His handsome, boyish looks, combined with a successful publicity campaign, have helped endear him to millions of Americans, most of whom know him through his appearances in two motion pictures, *The Turning Point* (1977) and *White Nights* (1985), and a nationally televised special, *Baryshnikov on Broadway* (1980).

As a leading dancer in his homeland, Baryshnikov enjoyed the most privileged status attainable in Soviet society next to that of leading politicians. His discontent with Soviet life seems to have been based solely on ar-

Mikhail Baryshnikov sought artistic rather than political freedom when he defected to the West while on tour in Canada in 1974. He eventually became an American citizen.

Upholding the grand tradition of Russian ballet, Natalia Makarova has brought the excellence of her training at Leningrad's Kirov Ballet to the spotlight of the world's stages since her defection in 1970.

tistic grounds, leading him to declare soon after his arrival in America: "No other country in the world will be my home but Russia. You can be a citizen anywhere, but my soul will always be a Russian one."

Through sharing and reinterpretation, the culture that Russian immigrants brought to America has been sustained and embellished. Whether expressed in Russian, English, or the universal languages of music, art, and dance, Russian cultural life continues. And the arrival of the latest immigrants from Russia further enhances the Russian-American, and the American, heritage. ✎

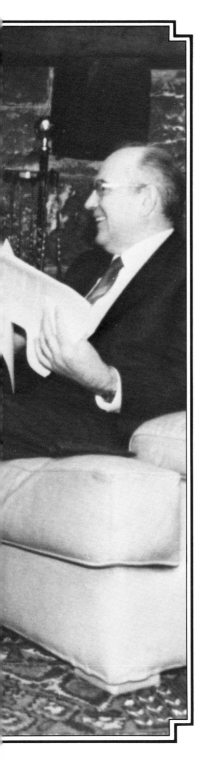

Ronald Reagan and Mikhail Gorbachev held five summit meetings in the late 1980s to discuss nuclear-arms reductions, human rights, and increased emigration from the USSR.

IMPROVING RELATIONS

Russians lived in North America even before the United States became a nation. During the past century, when they began to arrive in large numbers, Russian immigrants have left an indelible mark on the New World.

Most immigrants left the homeland because of unfavorable conditions, including economic hardship, religious persecution, civil war, the establishment of the Soviet government, a foreign invasion, involuntary displacement, and limited prospects for the future. Most immigrants saw America as their salvation. Yet, despite their general success, after settling in Russians have faced a dilemma.

Often viewed as communist or at least un-American when they arrive, they seek to counter that image without abandoning their traditions. But labels can be hard to alter. A further difficulty awaits the newest immigrants, most of whom are Jews but neither religiously committed nor accepted by the older non-Jewish Russian immigrants and their descendants. And for those

Russian Jews who are observant, the religious practices they kept alive in a hostile Soviet Union were not always fully in line with religious practices in the United States. In either case, the major question remains: Will these latest Russian Americans successfully integrate with the older immigrants, retaining a strong ethnic identity, or will they choose greater assimilation into American society?

Beginning in the mid-1980s, Soviet citizens received greater political freedoms, including a relaxation in emigration quotas. For the first time, Gorbachev's government also allowed emigrants to return to the homeland for up to several weeks to visit relatives. Thousands of Russian Americans took advantage of the opportunity. Some post-1970 immigrants, disillusioned with life in America, requested and received permission to return to the Soviet Union.

Now that the Soviet Union has been dismantled, Russians are finding it easier than ever to travel abroad,

Three generations of Russian Americans in rural Marion County, Oregon: Panfil Sengiriv, his son-in-law Vasil Cam, and Cam's son Josef.

to emigrate, and to revisit the homeland. Families separated for years, even decades, are being reunited. And now that the superpowers are no longer engaged in ideological warfare, immigrants from Russia are no longer automatically associated with communism. They can be recognized for what they are: people from a complex country seeking a new life in America and, in the process, making American society more diverse. ❧

FURTHER READING

Aksyonov, Vasily. *In Search of Melancholy Baby.* Translated by Michael Heim and Antonina Bouis. New York: Random House, 1987.

Billington, James. *The Icon and the Axe: An Interpretive History of Russian Culture.* New York: Vintage, 1970.

Chevigny, Hector. *Russian America: The Great Alaska Adventure, 1741–1867.* Portland, OR: Binford & Mort, 1979.

Davis, Jerome. *The Russian Immigrant.* New York: Arno Press, 1969.

Ignatieff, Michael. *The Russian Album.* New York: Viking Press, 1987.

Jeletzky, T. F., ed. *Russian Canadians: Their Past and Present.* Ottawa, Ontario: Borealis Press, 1983.

Kochan, Lionel, and Richard Abraham. *The Making of Modern Russia* (revised ed.). New York: Penguin Books, 1983.

Matich, Olga, and Michael Heim, eds. *The Third Wave: Russian Literature in Emigration.* Ann Arbor: Ardis, 1984.

Ripp, Victor. *Moscow to Main Street: Among the Russian Emigres.* Boston: Little, Brown, 1984.

Sevela, Efraim. *Why There Is No Heaven on Earth.* New York: Harper & Row, 1982.

Woodcock, George, and Ivan Avakumovic. *The Doukhobors.* Toronto and New York: Oxford University Press, 1968.

INDEX

PAUL ROBERT MAGOCSI is professor of history and of political science at the University of Toronto, where he holds the chair of Ukrainian Studies. His many publications include *The Shaping of a National Identity: Subcarpathian Rus', 1848-1948; Galicia: A Historical Survey and Bibliographical Guide; Our People: Carpatho-Rusyns and Their Descendants in North America;* and *Ukraine: A Historical Atlas*. He also served as research editor, map editor, and author of several entries in the *Harvard Encyclopedia of American Ethnic Groups*.

SANDRA STOTSKY is director of the Institute on Writing, Reading, and Civic Education at the Harvard Graduate School of Education as well as a research associate there. She is also editor of *Research in the Teaching of English,* a journal sponsored by the National Council of Teachers of English.

Dr. Stotsky holds a bachelor of arts degree with distinction from the University of Michigan and a doctorate in education from the Harvard Graduate School of Education. She has taught on the elementary and high school levels and at Northeastern University, Curry College, and Harvard. Her work in education has ranged from serving on academic advisory boards to developing elementary and secondary curricula as a consultant to the Polish Ministry of Education. She has written numerous scholarly articles, curricular materials, encyclopedia entries, and reviews and is the author or co-author of three books on education.

REBECCA STEFOFF is a writer and editor who has published more than 50 nonfiction books for young adults. Many of her books deal with geography, environmental issues, and exploration, including the three-volume set *Extraordinary Explorers*. She has worked with Ronald Takaki in adapting *Strangers from a Distant Shore* into a 15-volume Chelsea House series, the ASIAN AMERICAN EXPERIENCE. Stefoff studied English at the University of Pennsylvania, where she taught for three years. She lives in Portland, Oregon.

REED UEDA is associate professor of history at Tufts University. He graduated summa cum laude with a bachelor of arts degree from UCLA, received master of arts degrees from both the University of Chicago and Harvard University, and received a doctorate in history from Harvard.

Dr. Ueda was research editor of the *Harvard Encyclopedia of American Ethnic Groups* and has served on the board of editors for *American Quarterly, Harvard Educational Review, Journal of Interdisciplinary*

History, and *University of Chicago School Review.* He is the author of several books on ethnic studies, including *Postwar Immigrant America: A Social History, Ethnic Groups in History Textbooks,* and *Immigration.*

DANIEL PATRICK MOYNIHAN is the senior United States senator from New York. He is also the only person in American history to serve in the cabinets or subcabinets of four successive presidents–Kennedy, Johnson, Nixon, and Ford. Formerly a professor of government at Harvard University, he has written and edited many books, including *Beyond the Melting Pot, Ethnicity: Theory and Experience* (both with Nathan Glazer), *Loyalties,* and *Family and Nation.*

Picture Credits